ENDANGERED HARVEST

The Future of Bay Area Farmland

The Report of the Farmlands Conservation
Project of People for Open Space
November 1980

Credits

People for Open Space (POS) is a Bay Area-wide non-profit citizen conservation organization. Memberships in POS are welcomed; information is provided on the last page. The POS Farmlands Conservation Project was a two-year study supervised by the following special committee:

Allan B. Jacobs, Chairman and POS President

Leslie Ayers
Joseph Bodovitz
William Devlin
Barbara Eastman
Volker Eisele
Dorothy Erskine
William D. Evers

James Hobbs
Marguerite K. Johnston
T. J. Kent, Jr.
Lawrence Livingston, Jr.
Michael Marston
Sylvia McLaughlin
Clem Shute

Larry Orman, Project Director

Funding for the Farmlands Project was provided primarily through grants from the Packard, Gerbode and Columbia foundations and the Haas Fund.

Design & Production by Philip DiLernia & Lisa Vincent/
Production Asst., Chris Windle

Typesetting by petrographics/typeworld

Printing by Fremont Litho, Inc.

Cover Photo by Joe Samberg

Back & Inside Cover Photos by William Garnett

Photography: Dan Brody, Richard Conrat/BCDC, William Garnett, Barry Rokeach, Joe Samberg/Oakland Museum, Santa Rosa News Herald: all other photos by Larry Orman. (All photos are copyrighted.)

People for Open Space
46 Kearny Street
San Francisco, CA 94108
(415) 781-8729

ISBN: 0-9605262-0-X

Contents

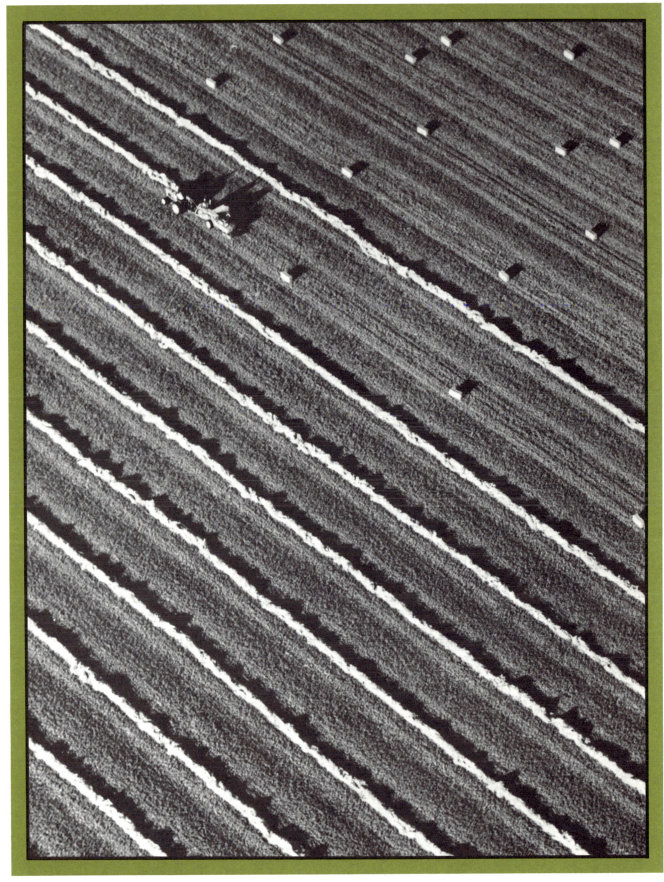

Barry Rokeach

Introduction

What kind of place is the Bay Area for farming?

What is happening to farmland here?

How do people in cities benefit by having farms and ranches near them?

These are some of the questions asked and answered by the Farmlands Conservation Project, a two-year undertaking of the regional organization People for Open Space. This book, addressed to all the citizens of the Bay Area, is the Project's final report.

The Farmlands Project is a first of its kind. Never before has a major research project looked at Bay Area agricultural land — not just as a form of open space on which incidentally some crops are grown, but for its essential value as *food-producing land*. In fact, few thorough studies of agriculture in metropolitan regions have been made in the United States. An account of the project, and a description of its six major background reports and other technical papers and special studies are included as an appendix at the end of this summary report.

People for Open Space sees this project as contributing to its long-standing goal: the creation of a permanent Greenbelt for the nine counties of the Bay Area. And that idea requires some explanation.

For over 200 years the open land of the Bay Area has served the people who live here. It has been garden and ranch, woodlot and quarry, watershed and game preserve. Within it we have built a major metropolis that now requires more in resources than our nine counties alone can provide. But the richness close to home is still a major support for life in the Bay Area, and one of the things that makes Bay Area living good.

Over the years we have learned to value our remaining natural landscape. We have protected key elements: our magnificent parks, our watersheds, our habitat reserves, our open Bay and tidelands.

But this progress has not kept pace with change. The metropolis, once contained in a few compact centers, now has outposts, extensions, and influences in every corner of the Bay Area. What was a collection of separate cities and towns has become a single urban organism, a supercity. There is grandeur in this, but danger also: the city threatens to overwhelm the countryside.

Compared with this rushing-outward of the metropolis, our land-preserving efforts have been like a cottage industry competing with an assembly-line. No longer is it enough to save, by special effort, a fragment here, a fragment there. The *system* of developed areas must have a counterpart: a *system* of protected open lands.

REGIONAL PLAN OPEN SPACE SYSTEM

Adapted from the ABAG Regional Plan 1970: 1990

SONOMA

NAPA

SOLANO

MARIN

San
Pablo
Bay

CONTRA COSTA

SAN FRANCISCO

San
Francisco
Bay

ALAMEDA

N
W——E
S

SAN
MATEO

Open Space System
3.4 million acres permanent,
plus 628,000 acres for
after-1990 urbanization — only if
population exceeds 7.2 million

Urban Areas to 1990
Based on 1970 projection of 7.2
million people by 1990 —
current projections are for a
maximum of 6.2 million
by 2000

Scale in Miles   0   5   10   20

We must establish, coequal with the metropolis and surrounding it, a Greenbelt: a coherent and permanent structure of open land. Only thus can the Bay Area's land continue to serve us: to produce a portion of our food; to supply high-quality water; to reduce the threat from floods and other hazards; to maintain the richness of plant and animal life; to give us room to wander and to breathe. Of equal importance, such a Greenbelt would serve our cities by the very fact of setting bounds to them. It would protect their character as distinct urban places: places to which we can feel we belong.

But if the protection of farmland is a needed step toward creating a Bay Area greenbelt, it has an added importance of its own. Farmland loss due to urban growth is now a recognized national problem. Our region — and every region rich in agricultural land — has a responsibility to protect its share of this superb but dwindling national resource.

Today, in the matter of farmland, the people of the Bay Area have a chance to take charge of a part of their future: to halt a destructive trend and establish in its place a pattern that makes sense for the long haul. We think that's an opportunity too good, and too rare, to be missed.

1 Save The Farmbelt!

Fifteen years ago the cry was: "Save the Bay!" Maybe it's time for a new slogan, a big bright sticker on Bay Area bumpers: "Save the Farmbelt!"

Around our Bay Area cities lies a treasure we have only dimly recognized: a belt of highly productive agricultural land. Before our region became the fifth-largest metropolitan area in the country, it was a major food producer. It *still is*. These nine counties yield more value in foodstuffs each year than thirteen entire states, including New Jersey, the "Garden State"; they produce half as much as Oregon. The total annual value of the region's crops now stands at $750 million. Regional farms and ranches employ 60,000 people and add an estimated $2 billion to the regional economy.

The Farmbelt is big business; it is more. Like the waters of the Bay itself, the farmlands mark one edge of the metropolis. Like the Bay, they are good to look at. Like the Bay, they help make our region one of the nation's most liveable and most admired. But there is this important difference: while the Bay is well protected now, the farmlands are without protection still.

And the Farmbelt is shrinking. Of 2.8 million acres of agricultural land in the region in 1949, about 708,000 have gone out of production since. Another 19,000 acres — a chunk two thirds the size of San Francisco — shuts down every year. Three quarters of that loss, at least, is due to urban growth and its effects. And the shrinkage shows no sign of slowing down. Rather, it is gaining speed.

For years we have put up with farmland loss, here and nationwide. "Too bad," the common reaction was, "but what can you do about it?"

But the world is waking up to a cold reality: total world food supply today is barely equal to total consumption. And worldwide and nationwide the attitude is changing. "Ten years from now," says a Soil Conservation Service official, "Americans could be as concerned over the loss of the nation's prime and important farmlands as they are today over the shortages of oil and gasoline." Already the word is spreading: Farmland loss is no longer an accepted, acceptable thing.

Stopping it, of course, is another matter. But across this nation and others, methods of protecting agricultural land are being tested and applied.

Dan Brody

In North America, British Columbia and the State of Oregon have taken the strongest action. California is among the many states that have done nothing much at all.

It's not that the public doesn't know the score. Here in the Bay Area, a recent Field poll found 71 percent of the people questioned in favor of saving high-quality farmland; 78 per cent said that the horizontal sprawl of cities should be slowed. Rich and poor, black and white and Chicano, felt the same way by the same high margins.

But California governments have had trouble responding to this mood. The Legislature has considered the issue but seems unlikely to take strong action soon. Local governments frequently endorse the idea of protecting farmland, and have, in some cases, succeeded in slowing the loss. But present efforts, judged by the results, are not enough. Ordinances pass, votes are taken, environmental impact reports written — and the Farmbelt shrinks all the while.

Sometime within the next few decades, as national farmland loss matures from "problem" to "crisis," federal action no doubt will come. But in the Bay Area we have little time to wait. Much of the best of our farmland is up for grabs right now; and much of our Farmbelt is likely to be left out of any broad-brush protection plan mandated from Washington.

In brief, this is what we propose:

The State Legislature should establish a temporary Agricultural Land Commission for the nine Bay Area counties. Its charge: to study regional agriculture and its needs and, in the meantime, to hold intact as much farmland as possible. After two years, the Commission would propose a plan for the future protection of the Farmbelt, including any necessary measures to support the business of farming. It

Richard Conrat/BCDC

would then be up to the people of the region: a nine-county election would be held to vote the proposal up or down.

There may be another formula: there may be a better answer: but an answer there must be. It is time for all ideas to be brought forward. It is time for the Farmland debate to begin.

The Bay Area's Farmbelt

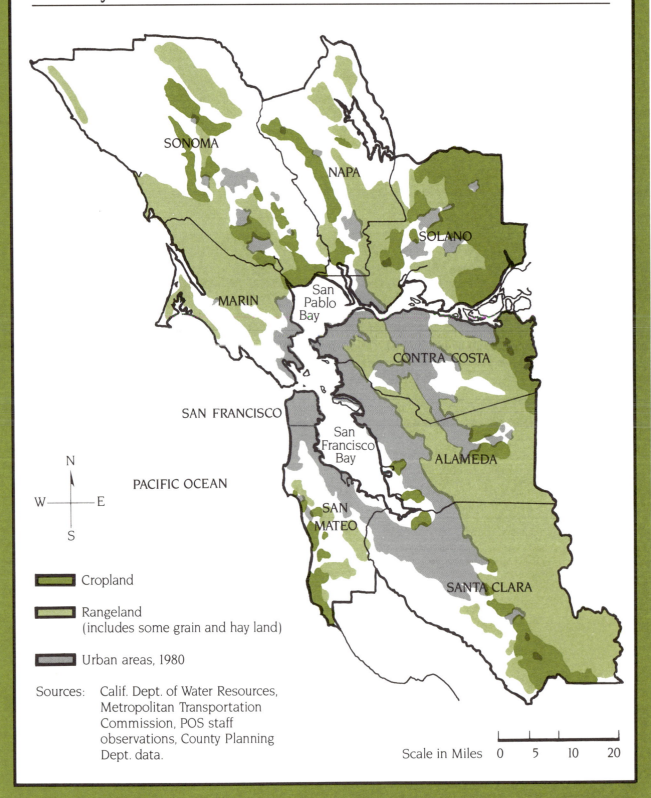

SONOMA

NAPA

SOLANO

MARIN

San
Pablo
Bay

CONTRA COSTA

SAN FRANCISCO

San
Francisco
Bay

ALAMEDA

N
W — E
S

PACIFIC OCEAN

SAN
MATEO

SANTA CLARA

Cropland

Rangeland
(includes some grain and hay land)

Urban areas, 1980

Sources: Calif. Dept. of Water Resources,
Metropolitan Transportation
Commission, POS staff
observations, County Planning
Dept. data.

Scale in Miles   0   5   10   20

2 The Living Farmbelt

What kind of place is the Bay Area for farming?

John Marsh, who ranched in Contra Costa County a hundred years ago, had a pretty good answer: "Particularly in the vicinity of San Francisco's Bay," he wrote, "most extraordinary crops are raised with very negligible cultivation."

The modern farmer would scoff at the word "negligible." But the fact remains that this is an excellent place to grow food. Three of these counties — Solano, Sonoma, and Santa Clara — are among the top 100 in the nation in value of agricultural sales. Per-acre value of most crops is near the California average — which runs among the highest in the world. The Farmbelt grows almost every product California does — over 100 crops, 38 of them grossing over $1 million in sales. Some of those foodstuffs can only be raised in coastal areas.

THE LAND

The nine counties have about 4.5 million acres of land within their boundaries; 90 percent of that was originally good for some kind of agriculture. Even now, agriculture is the largest single use of land: over two million acres, almost half of the region's area. It is an empire: 49,000 acres in vegetables, 120,000 in orchards and vineyards, 289,000 in field crops (mostly grains for animal fodder) and, surrounding it all, fully 1.6 million acres of pasture and range. In 1979 this land gave us over 100,000 tons of apples, 19,000 tons of lettuce, 628 million eggs, 715,000 tons of tomatoes, 100 million gallons of milk and cream — to begin a long list: a regional harvest worth three quarters of a billion dollars.

Climate is part of the local edge. Like most of California, the Bay Area has a long growing season. Unlike interior regions, we have a summer moderated by the influence of fog. As days grow hot inland, the inland air warms and rises; to replace it sea air flows from the coast, carrying fog with it.

This cycle brings cool, moist overcast to the immediate coastline almost daily, more rarely to the inland valleys. Mountain barriers and passes let the fog into one valley, exclude it from the next. We thus have many climates, not one. In different parts of the region the weather favors leafy vegetables,

BAY AREA FARMLAND BY COUNTY — 1974*

Counties	Vegetable Crops	Field Crops	Fruits & Nuts	Total Cultivated	Range & Pasture	Total Farmland	% Of Land Area
Alameda	3,018	26,837	3,641	33,496	213,277	264,773	56%
Contra Costa	7,678	30,907	11,600	50,185	198,832	249,017	53
Marin	3	4,800	82	4,885	127,074	131,959	40
Napa	26	12,490	21,661	34,177	174,950	209,127	43
San Mateo	2,050	9,616	516	12,182	58,988	71,170	25
Santa Clara	14,245	17,743	20,410	52,398	327,955	380,353	45
Solano	21,843	140,891	17,605	180,339	186,378	366,717	68
Sonoma	184	45,592	44,476	90,252	423,889	514,141	51
Region	49,047	288,876	119,991	457,914	1,729,343	2,187,257	49%

*Nursery acreage not included. Estimated at 10,000 acres.

(Source: 1974 Census of Agriculture)

flowers, grapes, dairies, apples, cherries, or range cattle.

Good soil helps. Though topsoil forms slowly — as slowly as one inch in 10,000 years — some of our valleys have topsoil thirty-five feet deep. (We have not been careful with this lavish, irreplaceable resource: these valley lands are the ones we have built over first and fastest.)

By acreage, though, the bulk of the region's agricultural land is in the rugged hills: not farms growing crops but ranches producing milk, meat, and wool. In fact, ours is the one area of California where the coastal ranges are predominantly grassy, rather than forested or brush-covered. Our 1.6 million acres of range and pastureland form an almost continuous expanse within which both cities and cultivated areas appear as enclaves. Cattle and other livestock produce almost a third of the region's annual farm income.

To dismiss this as "merely" grazing land is a big mistake. In fact, Bay Area rangeland is three times as productive as the California average. One range conservationist lists the area "among the most productive in the U.S." Again it's the fog that does it. The closer to the coast, the longer the season is during which animals can be grazed directly on the land, without imported fodder. This gives the local dairyman or beef-cattle rancher a definite advantage. In the Sierra or Central Valley, it may take twenty acres of range to support one cow and her calf; near Livermore or Fairfield the same pair can live on ten

THE PRODUCTIVITY OF BAY AREA RANGELAND

County	acres of range	AUM's*	AUM's/acre
Alameda	250,000	175,000	1.0
Contra Costa	175,000	232,000	0.9
Marin	145,000	83,000	0.6
Napa	207,000	295,000	1.4
San Mateo	37,000	44,000	1.2
Santa Clara	229,000	209,000	0.9
Solano	175,000	175,000	1.0
Sonoma	200,000	400,000	2.0
Region total	1,418,000	1,613,000	1.1

Other Regions	acres of range	AUM's*	AUM's/acre
Western Sierra	2,153,000	1,315,000	0.6
San Joaquin Valley	7,229,000	3,402,000	0.5
Southern Calif.	6,286,000	1,069,000	0.2
California total	35,968,000	12,918,000	.36

*AUM's produced by range only   Source: Reed, U.C. Agricultural Extension (1974)

Note: AUM means Animal Unit Month, the amount of feed required by a cow and a calf for a month.

acres; but in much of the East Bay Hills and the Marin-Sonoma coastlands, it takes as little as six acres. This is extraordinary.

The Farmbelt is no seamless expanse. Each county, each subregion is different. There are specialties and linked communities. The dairy ranchers, for instance, know each other; trade advice and skills; use the same suppliers. County lines don't quite match the natural compartments of Bay Area agriculture, but each county, seen as part of the Farmbelt, has a character of its own.

THE FARMS AND THE FARMERS

Think of California agriculture and you visualize mile upon mile of alfalfa or olives or rice — the enormous monocultures of the Central Valley, often run by major agricultural corporations. In most of the Bay Area the pattern is different. In this varied landscape, few ownerships get very large. Though some operations, like cattle ranches, need a lot of acres by nature, the trend is not toward ever greater expansion. Few Bay Area firms are run by large corporations. (It is not uncommon, however, for family farms to incorporate for business reasons; 350 Bay Area farms have done so.)

In 1974 there were over 7,000 farms in the Bay Area. But about 1,600 of them yielded 90 percent of the produce (measured by dollar sales). These make up the mainstream of regional agriculture.

Bay Area farmers are older, on the average, than the population as a whole. Their average age is now 54. But it hasn't changed much since 1959 and is almost identical to statewide and national figures. There are as many *young* farmers, proportionately, as ever. So the conventional belief that farmers are a "dying breed" simply does not hold.

Farmers tend to have strong family ties; they cluster by national origin. Many flowergrowers and orchardists are Japanese; a lot of San Mateo vegetable growers are Italian and Portuguese. Dairymen everywhere seem to run to Italian surnames. The ancestors of today's owners typically arrived in this country unskilled and went to work as farm laborers.

BAY AREA FARMS
BY ECONOMIC CLASS

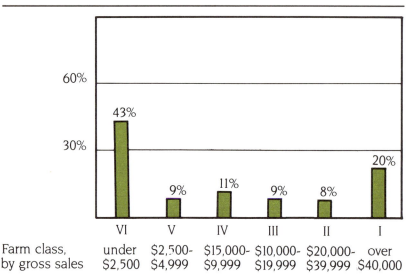

Farm class, by gross sales	VI under $2,500	V $2,500- $4,999	IV $15,000- $9,999	III $10,000- $19,999	II $20,000- $39,999	I over $40,000
	43%	9%	11%	9%	8%	20%

Source: U.S. Census of Agriculture (1974)

For of course it takes more than farmers to keep agriculture going: it takes hired workers by the thousands. A dairy ranch may have three or four hired hands year round, a cauliflower farm several hundred workers at harvest time. About 60,000 people are employed on farms for some period each year. Most are Mexican, Latino, Filipino, or Portuguese. With farm work becoming more complex and exacting, much of it must now be considered at least semi-skilled.

HOW ARE
THEY DOING?

How profitable is Bay Area farming? Statistics give no direct answer. In most areas, farmers seem to be doing as well as their colleagues outside the region. The costs of water, labor, and credit are all within normal ranges. Yields run from fair to excellent.

Farming isn't an easy business. It never has been. That's true nationwide. It is fair to say that Bay Area farmers have their share of the standard

problems — plus some additional ones caused by urban encroachment. It is distinctly *not* valid to claim — as some have done — that local agriculture is inherently incapable of sustaining itself; that it just doesn't pay.

One genuine problem is the price of land. Ideally, farmland should sell at prices that farmers can pay, over some years, from the income the land produces. But this balance point is long since past, both locally and nationwide. Even when both buyer and seller are farmers, farmland often sells at prices too high to be paid from farm income alone.

Farmland is widely considered to be a good investment. It makes a fine tax shelter, for one thing. And it has a history of increasing in value faster than inflation takes value away. Farmers themselves are very aware of this, and look for chances to expand their holdings. They regard land as retirement insurance; even if they only sell to other farmers, they will walk away with a good piece of cash. For all these reasons, the market in farmland is a seller's market; prices continue to rise.

For the farmer who already owns considerable land, this escalation is an advantage. For someone who is trying to buy a first property, however, or to expand from a small base, high prices are an increasing obstacle. In the long run, extreme price escalation has to be seen as a threat to continued farming. When the possibility of development adds a speculative element, prices climb radically and the economic threat to continued farming is immediate.

Inheritance taxes — mainly Federal — make trouble for farmers everywhere.

Often heirs must sell their land to pay the cost of inheriting it! High land prices, reflected in these taxes, increase the pressure. Year-to-year property taxes, by contrast, are much less of a burden after Proposition 13 — particularly if the farmer makes use of the Williamson Act.

The small size of Bay Area farms both helps and hurts. It hurts, because small growers have less power in the marketplace and face some proportionately higher operating costs. It helps, because the small farmer can oversee his operation more closely than his corporate competitors. Often the result is higher quality. Though a better product does not always mean a better price, the potential is certainly there.

Safeway, for instance, gives bonuses for high-quality local milk; some local forage growers produce a premium cattle feed that is in high demand; and there are proposals to establish a "supergrade" class in fresh produce. In the Santa Clara Valley locally grown tomatoes are generally of very high quality, an advantage for many processors.

Some types of agriculture currently have special problems. In parts of Sonoma County and Santa Clara County, old unproductive orchards must now be torn out and replaced with more profitable crops. This is an expensive process.

GENERAL FARM TYPES BY SIZE

Major Product	Related Products	Bay Area Common Size Range (est.)*
Beef cattle	Forage crops	500-10,000 ac.
Vineyards	—	25-250 ac.
Vegetables Fruits & Nuts	Often mixed	25-1,000 ac.
Greenhouses, Field Flowers	—	5-50 ac.
Field crops	Often mixed with other crops	100-1000 ac.
Dairy	Forage	400-1,000 ac.

*Will vary greatly due to leasing and weather   Source: POS staff estimates

Such shifting from crop to crop, however, is a part of agricultural life. (The Napa Valley was once planted chiefly to wheat!) Local combinations of climate and soil frequently permit many different crops to be grown on the same land, and this often makes crop shifting easier.

The beef-cattle business is tougher than most. Profits are less regular and lower than for farming in general; herd size and income rise and fall in a multi-year pattern called the "cattle cycle." At the bottom of the curve, inevitably, some operators are hurting. In the Bay Area, it takes about 2000 acres to produce a good fulltime ranch income; many owners have less land and combine part-time ranch work with other

employment. But these difficulties are generally no greater than in other ranching regions; and for stock raisers as for other farmers, the land itself has been an inflation-beating asset.

Perhaps the worst problem facing the Bay Area rancher or farmer is the special kind of uncertainty that goes with farming in an urban region. Will his land still be in agriculture five years, ten years, or twenty years hence? Will the city reach out his way? Will the purchase offer that can't be refused — half dreaded, half anticipated — come this year, next year, or never? Faced with such doubts, farmers may hesitate to make the major investments in equipment, improvements, or livestock that long-range success in agriculture requires.

If that uncertainty can be removed, Bay Area agriculture, in most areas and in most crops, will prove robust. Where problems remain, public and private actions can combine to solve them — once we recognize that our agriculture is, in fact, an asset too excellent not to defend.

FOCUS: The Crops of the Counties

Art Rogers

Joe Samberg/Oakland Museum

Marin County

Marin, like San Mateo has cities east and agriculture west; and here, too, the fog is all-important. Instead of flowers and vegetables, the leading product is milk (along with some beef and wool). The rolling hills and lowlands of western Marin are superlative diary country. A few spots in eastern Marin near Novato along the Bay, are planted to hay and silage crops — food for the cows of the western dairy ranches.

San Mateo County

Open-air farming is long since gone from the bay side of San Mateo County (though greenhouses remain). The Coastside, though, has the regon's most specialized cropland. Here, under all but continuous fog, is the place for crops that want it wet and cool. From the Coastside come artichokes and Brussels sprouts, along with field flowers, mushrooms, grains, pumpkins, peas and other vegetables. This is the Bay Area's slice of California's fogbelt, a farmland resource of national significance. San Mateo has also considerable grazing lands on its mountainous central spine, interspersed in the south with large areas of forest.

Sonoma County

Sonoma County is an agricultural powerhouse. In its foggy dairylands, it outdoes Marin: the low rolling South Merced Hills, along the Marin line, have some of the state's best grazing land. Petaluma is the market and service center for dairies in both counties. The central valley of the county, from Petaluma to Santa Rosa and Healdsburg, supports the dairies by producing oat hay, silage corn, and other forage crops. More forage is grown on the diked-off marshlands along the Bay's rim, especially at Tubbs Island.

Elsewhere, Sonoma grows mostly fruit. Along the western rim of the central plain lies the Sebastopol apple belt, where some 8000 acres of orchards yield over 100,000 tons of apples for eating and canning each year. Some berries are grown in the same region.

Farther from the coast lie the vineyards: in the Dry Creek Valley and the Alexander Valley; in the Sonoma Valley to the east; and in Knights and Franz Valleys near Mount St. Helena. Vineyards covered 24,000 acres in 1979 and — unlike most crops — are still expanding.

Sonoma has also large areas grazed by beef cattle and sheep — notably on Sonoma Mountain. And it has vast areas that are neither farm nor ranch nor city, but forest.

Napa County

Like Sonoma, Napa County is patterned by north-south valleys; like Marin, it has a dominant product: wine. The rich and well-drained volcanic soil — unusual in the region — is superb for grapes. So is the climate. In the Napa Valley and the remoter Pope and Chiles Valleys, forty different grape varieties are grown on almost 25,000 acres. Livestock is the second major product: large areas along the Bay near American Canyon and in the eastern hills are grazed.

Contra Costa County

Contra Costa County once had three important cropland belts: the rich Bay Plain on the west; the deep-soiled interior valley between the Berkeley Hills and Mount Diablo; and, on the east, a fringe of land near Brentwood that belongs geographically to the Central Valley. Today, only these East County farms remain — about 30,000 acres, largely in fruits and nuts (with some tomatoes, lettuce, asparagus, barley, corn and hay). Farther east, toward the Delta, salinity and flooding problems restrict the land to shallow-rooted grains like barley and field corn.

The rest of the county, on either side of the suburban Diablo Valley, is grazing land, and much of that is superb. In the Tassajara Hills, near the southern county line, the rolling rangeland is so rich that it can also support grain crops.

Solano County

The Bay Area counties don't end precisely where the Coast Ranges do. Several include within their boundaries some of the floor of California's agricultural empire, the Central Valley. Solano has the largest chunk. Around Dixon are 75,000 acres of the best types of land — Class I and Class II soils. Most of this land is in sugar beets, field corn, and tomatoes. South toward the Delta, a second vast farm area is mostly in sugar beets, with some grains and hay. Again south, along the Sacramento River channel, rise the low Montezuma Hills — grazed, and intermittently planted to wheat and barley. West of the Montezuma country, forage crops are grown around the north rim of the Suisun Marsh. And all along the western rim of the county, in the lee of the Coast Ranges, lies a belt of grapes, pears, prunes, and almonds, with grazing on the grassy slopes above. The depth of the topsoil in parts of this area exceeds thirty-five feet.

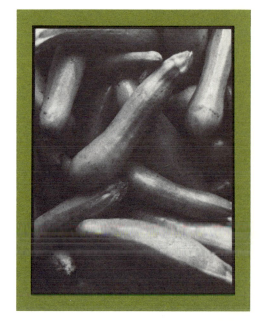

Joe Samberg/Oakland Museum

Alameda County

For almost sixty years the Bay Plain was the center of Alameda farming. On Bay Farm Island, and on the sites of San Leandro, Union City, and Fremont, fields of vegetables and orchards of cherries and apricots stretched for miles. Today, just one large area — the exceptional cauliflower and lettuce land on the North Plain of Fremont — remains (along with some greenhouse flower-growing).

Above the Bay Plain, in the Berkeley and Mission Hills, is some of the region's very special moist range-land. The growing season under the fog is long, the mixture of grasses good. Behind those hills lies the bowl of the Livermore Valley, surrounded on all sides by slopes of the Diablo Range.

Most of the rich floor grows grain and hay (some grapes as well). In the hills, the grazing is good near the Valley but only average in remoter parts; the back of the country of the Diablo Range is rugged, dry, and wild.

Joe Samberg/Oakland Museum

Joe Samberg/Oakland Museum

Santa Clara County

Most of Santa Clara County is hilly rangeland. The total number of beef cattle in the Santa Cruz and Diablo Ranges varies between 11,000—18,000 cows. But it is the central Santa Clara Valley that has been the scene of the county's most lucrative agriculture — and the scene of its loss. Since 1945 this county alone has seen the building-over of 170,000 acres of superlative soil. In the broad northern portion of the valley, only islands of farmland remain: on the bay plain near Sunnyvale; near the Los Gatos/Saratoga foothills; in the Evergreen/East San Jose area. Most significant is the Berryessa enclave west of Milpitas — the chief remaining area of vegetables and fruit. These still-valuable holdouts total about 10,000 acres and are shrinking fast. But further south, where the wide plain narrows to become the "South Valley," Bay Area agriculture has one of its strongholds: 55,000 acres of tomatoes, lettuce, cucumbers, bell peppers, and orchards. The cherry orchards of Santa Clara County are all but unique: this is one of the two spots in California ideally suited to them.

FOCUS: The Region's Farmers

What kind of people are the men and women who run the Bay Area's 1,600 commercially serious farms and ranches?

One word you have to use is *tough*. These farmers work harder than most people want to. They put up with more. Their affection for the land they work and the life they lead is deep but thoroughly unsentimental.

Take **Virginia Fellingham**. At nine, in Kansas, she was harrowing fields with a team of six horses. Now, with her daughter and son, she owns a 240-acre cattle ranch near Livermore and leases thousands of acres besides. "There were only ten years in my life," she says, "when I wasn't chasing a cow."

Fellingham is a small middle-aged woman in a blue chamois shirt and jeans, high boots for the farmyard mud, bandana at neck, glasses. She's stern and wry and talkative. Her great dislikes are permissiveness, off-road vehicles, and people who damage other people's property. She's seen disrespect for property in the hilly lands she leases; she's seen it closer to home. A neighborhood dog —"I know whose it is, but he won't believe it" — has just killed one of her lambs.

Fellingham could have chosen an easier business. Subject to weather, luck, and interest rates, it can cost $200 to $250 to raise a cow; a rancher may need to get $400 for that cow to keep the operation going and show an overall profit. Earnings tend to get plowed right back into the ranch. "This has to be a way of life," says Fellingham. "You have to love it. Who else would put up with it?"

In winter Fellingham can tell by the look of a slope what grasses are coming up. In summer she looks down with a certain smugness on the smog of Livermore: "I like it right here. It's so pretty in the morning . . . out here you don't need that stuff that keeps your mind straight." She gropes for the word, grins. "Tranquilizers, I mean."

Or take **Ralph Grossi**, Marin County dairyman. His family goes back a long way in these parts: Grossi's grandfather came here from Italian Switzerland in the 1890's and went to work as a milker. A generation later seven big Marin County ranches had the Grossi name on the sign out front. Ralph figures he's got 150 relatives within forty miles.

Ten years ago a neighboring ranch was sold and the Novato neighborhood of San Marin went up almost next door. "They told us our place would be one of the next to go," says Ralph. But Grossi was one of those who chose not to believe. Instead, he bought into the family partnership that owns this ranch and set to work running it.

Nor was Grossi content merely to hang on. He became a leader in the fight to create a different kind of future: one in which the demise of the ranches

would not be called inevitable. He is now President of the Marin County Farm Bureau; he is working to set up an Agricultural Land Trust to counter the trend toward disintegration of ranches. "People have to show politicians they're interested," he says.

Considering all this activity, it seems surprising that Grossi finds time to run a ranch. But run it he does, sometimes working sixteen-hour days. He likes this land, this 900-acre wedge of valley rising to boundary hills, and he's proud of his skill in using it.

Grossi foresees increasing competition between small family-run dairies like his and the vast corporate milk farms of the Central Valley. "There's going to be a big battle, to see whether or not the small dairies can succeed." But he is hopeful about the outcome. Small operations can concentrate on quality, giving their milk an extra appeal to some buyers. And Bay Area dairymen have another edge: the foggy coastal climate. For several months in a typical spring, cattle can live largely off the green land. Modest though it seems, this saving means a lot in the tight economy of a Marin ranch, where the feedbill can average $800 or more a day.

"When you start adding it up," says Grossi, "you've got to think that maybe in the long run it looks good."

A fairly recent recruit to the farming trade is **Jon Hudson**, who runs the Coastways Ranch on the San Mateo coast near Año Nuevo Point. Bearded, soft-voiced, self-contained, Hudson doesn't strike you as the farmer type. The son of an architect who raised grapes on the side, he grew up near Ukiah and worked for years as a surveyor and geologist. In 1965, relatives inherited shares in the farm on the coastal benchland south of Pescadero. Only Jon and Joan Hudson were interested in working it. "So there we were, with sixty acres of empty fields and no experience." After some difficult years, Jon knows his way with artichokes; now he's begun to vary his crops. He's added exotic-looking kiwi fruit and rows of Ollalie berries, blackberries of a large and succulent sort. Customers come to the ranch and pick berries from the vine: what's called a U-pick operation. "A moneymaker," Hudson says. He's not so sure about the profitability of the kiwis, though.

Here on the remote and rugged coast, the Hudsons have plenty of scenery: fog and cypresses and nearby ocean surf. They also have a bit of isolation to put up with. But Hudson doesn't seem to miss the city. On his weekly day off (if he gets around to it), he and Joan may drive to Santa Cruz, take in a movie, go folk-dancing. More often they stay at home. "And you can only read so long." Often by Sunday afternoon he's back out in the artichokes.

Mel and Steve Alameda, father and son, run a cauliflower farm. But that hardly says it. What they run is the thousand-acre Patterson Ranch, said to be some of the best cauliflower land in the state. And they run it within the city limits of rapidly-growing Fremont.

This is a big operation, a mechanized one. Equipment is everywhere. The fields are leveled for proper runoff by huge tractors guided by laser beams. The ranch employs, year-round, about one hundred workers, and another hundred in its own special packing plant downtown. Most are Mexican or Portuguese.

The Alamedas are themselves employees, and work for the L. S. Williams Company, which in turn leases the land from the owner, Patterson. This fact does not seem to lessen their farmerly attachment to the land. About their cauliflower they are frankly vain. Steve cuts a head with a sweep of the square-backed harvester's knife. It's massive, meaty, solid-looking, white as some heavy valuable foam. "Cauliflower from Salinas runs 22 pounds a crate," says Steve. "Ours runs 30 to 35 pounds."

Why such quality from these particular fields? "I'd say it's a good job of farming, but also it's the weather." Not too hot in summer, not too cold in winter, the East Bay Plain is one of the very few areas that are ideal for vegetables like cauliflower. "If you don't have the climate," says Steve Alameda, "you can't do anything."

Tom and Joe Furusho, brothers, have 400 acres of orchards and a packing plant in Sebastopol. Their father came to Sonoma County from Japan at the end of the last century and set to work as a laborer. Before long he had orchards of his own. The family rode out the 1930's on sheer hard work. "We've got seven people doing what my brother and I used to do," says Joe.

Then came Pearl Harbor and internment. The family was sent to Colorado; the land at home was lost. But Joe Furusho turned disaster into success. By sheer drive, he was able to farm successfully in Colorado. A few years later he came back to Sebastopol and recovered the family acreage and more.

"The apple business has been good to us," says Joe Furusho. But now he wonders. The cost of growing apples goes up all the time. And although some years are good, some bad, the profits are getting smaller. What puzzles the brothers, and angers them, is the gap between the farmer's price and the consumer's price. "We get 20¢ a pound for eating apples. I believe in profit, but you tell me why you have to pay 69¢?"

Up at the Furusho ranch, three generations of farming equipment rust or gleam. Out from the buildings spread orchards: old gnarled Gravensteins, up to a hundred years old and still bearing. Among the old trees, the Furushos have planted very young ones. "That's why it looks so crowded," Joe says as if challenged. "When we take the old ones out, the new ones will be right there."

Out in the trees — the new and the old — there's no sign yet of first spring flower. But if you know what to look for on a twig — if you know a little of what Joe Furusho knows — you'll know that the buds are thickening.

3
The Farmbelt And The City

Are the urban people of the Bay Area better off because they have the Farmbelt around them? Plainly.

Are the farmers better off because of the metropolis close by? In some ways they are, and the advantages will grow — if the cities can first be prevented from consuming the farms altogether.

In the cities, we tend to value the Farmbelt chiefly as open landscape — a very good reason; but we badly underestimate its most essential function: the production of *food*.

The Farmbelt as Garden

The producing power of this land is awesome. If all Bay Area cropland were planted to wheat, the harvest would potentially provide more than the amount of protein required by the current population of the region. If the suitable cropland was planted to tomatoes, the land could provide over a quarter of our protein needs (yes, tomatoes have protein!) along with more than half of the iron and almost four times the vitamin A that our five million people require. The region's dairylands contribute sixty percent of our milk supply, and the grazing lands add a moderate amount of meat protein.

The Farmbelt, of course, is not all wheat. It is not all anything. It grows not one crop but a hundred, and only a fraction of this diverse yield comes

to our own tables. But Bay Area people do eat better than the average city population — ask a visitor from New England! — and local production is part of the reason.

We get the benefit of the local specialities — Sebastopol apples, fogbelt artichokes, local wine. The produce we eat is largely local, with an extra edge of freshness. At certain seasons, fresh local crops bulk large in the produce bins: fruits like cherries, berries, apricots, and peaches; vegetables like lettuce, cabbage, spinach, artichokes, peas, pumpkins, and sweet corn. Fruit picked locally can be sold riper than fruit intended for long-range shipment. For the ultimate in freshness (short of the backyard garden) we have the chance to go direct — to pick Ollalie berries at a U-pick farm, even to rent a tree in an apple orchard.

For the farmer, the presence of a market of five million people close at hand can only be an advantage. All the milk and fresh vegetables grown locally are eaten here. Direct marketing — still something of a novelty — is very likely to grow in volume. Already there are seven farmers' markets in Bay Area towns, and five "Farm Trails" organizations linking over 150 U-pick farms and roadside stands for local produce. In

MAJOR BAY AREA PRODUCTS—SALES & ACREAGE (1979)

Product	Sales	Harvested Acres	$/acre	Leading County[1]
Alfalfa	$ 9,403,200	16,500	570	SOL (CC)
Almonds	4,092,500	6,526	627	SOL
Apples	17,127,000	7,857	2180	SON
Apricots	6,877,800	4,706	1461	SC, SOL (CC)
Artichokes	1,620,000	900	1800	SM
Barley	4,416,400	24,685	178	CC (SOL)
Beef cattle	65,781,600	—	—	SON (CC)
Brussels sprouts	3,000,000	1,100	273	SM
Cauliflower	5,020,000	2,555	1965	AL
Chickens	10,902,300	—	—	SON (AL, M)
Chinese vegetables	1,462,000	650	2249	SC
Corn, field	12,967,000	33,475	387	SOL
Corn, sweet	3,061,200	2,205	1388	SOL
Cucumbers	2,229,000	1,125	1981	SC
Eggs (all)	25,020,500	—	—	SON
Flowers and Foliage	119,206,600	—	—	SM (SC, AL)
Garlic	1,001,000	520	1925	SC
Grain	6,279,400	48,140	130	SON (M)
Grapes (all)	82,390,300	52,138	1580	NAPA (SON)
Hogs and Pigs	1,541,600	—	—	SON
Lettuce	2,913,000	1,753	1661	SC (CC)
Milk (all)	89,597,990	—	—	SON (M)
Mushrooms	14,514,000	93	156064	SC
Nursery	50,072,700	—	—	AL (SC)
Oats	2,754,500	14,050	196	SON
Pasture (irrigated)	3,832,000	44,175	87	SOL
Pears	6,847,000	5,974	1146	SOL
Peppers	4,683,400	2,557	1831	SC
Prunes	11,641,200	12,291	947	SON (SOL, CC)
Range	10,736,000	1,464,100	7	CC
Seeds	6,491,100	10,903	595	SOL (SC)
Sheeps & Lambs	7,729,950	—	—	SOL (SON)
Strawberries	3,686,000	300	12287	SC
Sugar Beets	20,799,300	22,375	788	SOL
Tomatoes	40,944,400	30,001	1365	SOL
Turkeys	2,473,100	—	—	SON
Walnuts	6,842,000	12,034	568	CC (SOL)
Wheat	17,651,500	48,240	364	SOL
Totals:	$687,608,540	1,876,180 ac.		Source: 1979 Agricultural Commissioners Reports

[1]In terms of gross sales value; counties with lesser, but significant sales are indicated in (   ).

San Francisco, Oakland, and San Jose, the Bay Area has four of the state's major produce terminals; these handle much more than local produce, but give the local farmer an easy outlet.

Several trends now underway suggest that this beneficial relation between city and farm — this symbiosis, so to speak — can become still closer.

Tastes in food are shifting. People value fresh fruits and vegetables more than ever before — just such produce as local agriculture is best at providing. Beef cattle raised on Bay Area grasslands, with little supplemental feed, yield leaner meat than cornfed cattle. Since many people these days are worried about eating too much fat, such meat should have an increasing market.

The price of energy goes up inexorably. More and more of the price of food reflects the energy cost of storing it and moving it long distances. Food that travels less and is consumed more quickly will be less expensive to deliver: a saving that should eventually mean higher profits for the grower or lower prices for the consumer.

This shortening of supply lines is already discernible in some cases. The cost of imported animal fodder from

BAY AREA AGRICULTURAL PRODUCTION 1979

County	Vegetables	Fruit & Nuts	Seed & Field Crops*	Livestock & Livestock Products**	Nursery	Totals
Alameda	10,387,000	2,910,000	5,092,000	10,017,700	31,775,000	$ 60,181,700
Contra Costa	11,058,400	7,310,670	13,521,700	16,828,750	15,713,800	64,433,320
Marin	—	72,000	2,122,000	33,263,050	1,264,900	36,721,950
Napa	156,000	41,153,200	1,093,000	10,912,500	3,436,000	56,750,700
San Mateo	17,806,000	210,000	1,278,000	1,911,300	67,501,000	88,706,300
Santa Clara	37,740,600	20,479,400	4,863,400	20,959,760	39,525,000	123,568,160
Solano	30,092,400	16,865,700	71,110,800	16,123,200	—	134,192,100
Sonoma	2,219,000	58,193,000	6,798,000	112,343,000	6,653,000	186,206,000
Region Totals	$109,459,400	$147,193,970	$105,878,900	$222,359,260	$165,868,700	$750,760,230

*Includes range and pasture
**Includes dairy and apiary

Source: 1979 *Agricultural Crop Reports* County Agricultural Commissioners

the Central Valley has gone so high that local dairymen and ranchers are developing local sources. Partly for this reason, the North Bay forage industry is rapidly expanding.

The Bay Area is by no means self-sufficient in food. No area of concentrated population can be. But our Farmbelt somewhat lessens our dependence on distant fields. And while we have it, we have also the possibility of greater self-reliance to come. If everything grown in the region were locally eaten, we could even now supply our own demand for fourteen crops. The region's farmland is highly adaptable: a given acre can grow any of several different foodstuffs. Fresh tomatoes, for instance — few of which are grown locally now — easily could be.

The Farmbelt as Industry

Looked at purely as an industry, our farmland makes a respectable contribution to the Bay Area economy. Its annual harvest is worth $750 million. In addition, Bay Area food processing plants employ 56,000 people, paying them $780 million. Although these plants process food from much of northern California, about a fifth of their raw material is local; many of them would leave the Bay Area if local production ceased. Because each dollar earned is spent and respent, the total value of agriculture in the regional economy in 1979 reached about $2 billion. Few other basic industries have so strong a ripple effect in the economy.

Dollars are dollars; but there are strong advantages to agriculture as a way of earning them. For one thing, this is a fairly stable industry. The demand for food, after all, can't fluctuate very widely. As a major newspaper's farm

FARM AND AGRICULTURAL-RELATED EMPLOYMENT 1976

County	Crop & Livestock Sales Value	Ag. Wage & Salary Employment	Farmers & Unpaid Family	Food Processing	Ag. Services	Total Ag. Employment	Total Wage & Salary Employment	% of Ag. & Related Employment
Alameda	$ 43,086,500	2,900	380	12,084	5,128	20,492	440,200	5%
Contra Costa	48,446,420	2,000	250	2,298	1,905	6,453	165,800	4
Marin	25,494,100	400	(NA)	128	674	1,202	58,100	2
Napa	31,733,300	2,400	380	927	73	3,780	29,100	13
San Francisco	0	400	(NA)	4,732	3,086	8,218	486,200	2
San Mateo	62,822,300	2,500	350	3,124	2,929	8,903	218,700	4
Santa Clara	97,347,450	7,400	1,330	9,643	4,282	22,655	499,800	5
Solano	88,494,200	3,100	750	1,412	320	5,582	61,900	9
Sonoma	127,058,800	4,000	1,070	2,110	1,098	8,278	70,200	12
Region	$ 524,482,070	25,100	4,510	36,458	19,495	85,653	2,030,000	4
State	$8,900,000,000	323,400	70,100	126,211	79,796	599,507	8,152,700	7

Sources: County Agricultlural Commissioner Reports, Calif.
Employment Development Dept. estimates.

reporter recently noted: "You can shut down an automobile assembly plant, but you can't lay off an orchard or a vineyard." Though farmers too suffer in a recession, the areas they live in are better off for their presence. To add to its stability, our agriculture is varied within itself. Bad weather may damage one crop, but rarely all.

It is common to see destructive activities defended simply because they provide employment. The debate over Redwood National Park came down to this one point: that preserving a certain acreage of redwoods might cause a certain number of loggers to lose their jobs. In the case of agriculture, there is no such conflict. To preserve the resource is to keep the jobs as well. As a cauliflower grower in Fremont remarks: "They're always trying to bring in industry. Well" (and he waves across his fields), "they've got a pretty good industry right here."

When fields are traded for tract houses (or ranches for ranchettes), it's an unlucky bargain for city budgets. When a new residential area is created, it requires government services; the increased property taxes collected from the land rarely cover the cost under our new tax rules. The tradeoff is particularly unfortunate for outlying towns — like Brentwood, Sebastopol, Gilroy — whose economies still largely depend on the farmland around them.

The Farmbelt and Water

Farms use about forty percent of the region's water supply. Because agriculture established its sources first, it relies mostly on traditional local water supplies; water imported from outside the Bay Area goes mostly to the expanding urban areas.

BAY AREA WATER USE

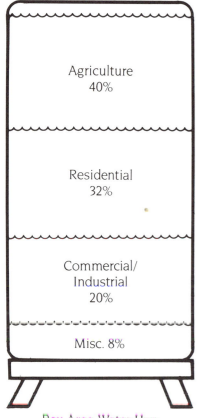

Bay Area Water Use
(1,585 mgd)

(mgd=million gallons per day)

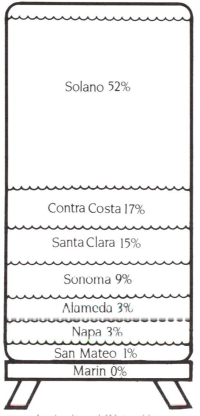

Agricultural Water Use
(645 mgd)

Source: ABAG Draft Water
Supply Plan (1977)

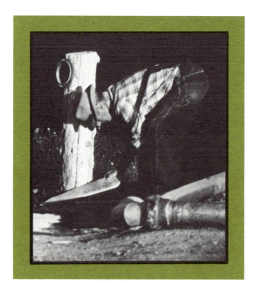

Though both cropland and cities use a lot of water per acre, developed areas consume more. In twenty years, at present rates of growth, the region will be pushing the limits of its present water supply. If farms must compete with cities for limited water, the price of water for cropland irrigation is likely to rise sharply. This possible competition, though, may be headed off by an elegant cooperative venture: one of those cases in which two seeming problems can be seen as the halves of one solution.

Bay Area sewage treatment agencies have a challenge to meet in this decade. Under federal water pollution laws, they must soon cease discharging partially treated effluent into inland waters like the Bay. Much of this effluent is non-toxic, but still rich in nutrients that, in water, act as pollutants. To correct the problems, sewage agencies have several choices, all expensive: they can, for instance, construct massive outfall pipes to dump effluent well out into the ocean, or add elaborate tertiary treatment. But among the alternatives is this one: to spread the effluent on cropland, where its nutrient content is, if anything, an advantage.

The irrigation of farmland with treated wastewater is now being tested on Sonoma County pastureland. (This new source of water accounts for part of the rapid increase in the North Bay forage industry.) At the moment, only about 5,000 acres in the Bay Area are getting such irrigation. But after the inevitable technical questions are worked out, far more land may be able to benefit. Most of the region's 400,000 acres of cropland could conceivably be getting reclaimed water some day.

Effluent irrigation is a fine example of the symbiosis that should occur between the cities and the farms. It certainly promises to lessen any competition for limited water supplies; it might even delay the day when new aqueducts and reservoirs are needed.

If, on the other hand, we allow our local agriculture to go out of business, we lose this opportunity. But there's more to it than that: the lost farmland would be replaced elsewhere, and the water cost of doing that would be high. If naturally arid lands in the Central Valley are brought under irrigation to replace Bay Area cropland, the total cost would be $56 million or more in water subsidies. It would cost a similar amount to replace Bay Area rangeland with irrigated pasture inland. The total amount of new water required would equal almost half the increased yield of the Peripheral Canal.

The Farmbelt and Clean Air

Much of our farmland lies in valleys that are natural pollution traps: the South Santa Clara Valley, the Livermore Valley, the Napa and Sonoma Valleys, and others. To trade the agriculture in such spots for development and its attendant air pollution seems a poor exchange in terms of human health and welfare. (Agriculture in the

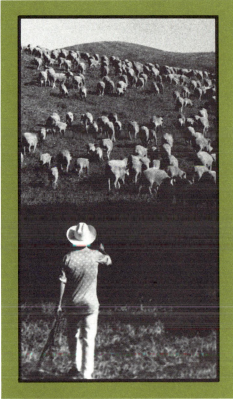

Bay Area is not an important contributor to air pollution. Agricultural burning is relatively small in scale and carefully controlled by environmental regulations.)

The Farmbelt as Landscape

The Farmbelt is half the Bay Area: half the landscape we live in. As landscape, it has special character. It gives us the particular sharp pleasure that comes from seeing land well used.

William Garnett

The Farmbelt's beauty has been praised by Jack London, Luther Burbank, and Robert Louis Stevenson, and many others. That beauty is a resource that we use heavily. Given a choice, we drive the highways that lead through farmland (such designated scenic roads as 580 and 680 in central Alameda County, Highway 1 in San Mateo County, and Highway 12 in Sonoma County get much of their charm from agricultural surroundings). We bicycle through the Farmbelt. We hike through it: at least 120,000 acres of park and watershed land, used basically for recreation, are also leased to cattle ranchers. The Farmbelt attracts tourists in large though uncounted numbers. (Christian Brothers Winery alone reports 300,000 visitors a year.) Hundreds of thousands of city people actually live in the Farmbelt for a few days or weeks each year: in vacation homes and cabins, summer camps and Scout camps, inns, hostel and commercial campsites. Such rural retreats are found among farms and ranches no less often than in wilder, forested country.

William Garnett

The Farmbelt contributes hugely to the image of our region as an extraordinary place to live. And that image must be listed as one of our most precious economic assets.

The Farmbelt landscape has a history, to be read not just in the occasional fine old barn or house, but on the land itself. Since agriculture began here two centuries ago, the crops and the scenery have changed many times. There was a period when cattle grazed everywhere, and a period when the Bay Area was the breadbasket for all California. Even now orchards are giving way to tomatoes, and rangeland to wine

William Garnett

grapes. The Farmbelt has adapted in the past; it will again.

The Farmbelt has another value: its ability to captivate and teach. Busloads of school children tour local farms and processing plants. More subtle, and possibly more effective, is the lesson taught by the experience of visiting a rural farm fair, or buying peaches at a farmers' market. In a time when the industries that sustain us are separated, distant, and sometimes incomprehensible, it is profoundly interesting to see close at hand where food comes from.

You might say that the Farmbelt brings us down to earth.

AGRICULTURAL FAIRS IN THE BAY AREA

Event	Location	Date	Attendance
Alameda Co. Fair	Pleasanton	6/24-7/8	404,153
Apple Blossom Festival	Sebastopol	4/11-13	
Calif. Spring Garden & Home Show	Oakland	4/29-5/6	11,637
Cloverdale Citrus Fair	Cloverdale	2/16-19	
Contra Costa Co. Fair	Antioch	8/1-5	62,415
Dixon May Fair	Dixon	5/9-13	47,007
Garlic Festival	Gilroy	8/2-3	25,000
Grand National Livestock Expo, Horseshow & Rodeo	San Francisco/ Daly City	10/26-11/4	143,228
Gravenstein Apple Festival	Sebastopol	8/9-10	
Harvest Hoedown	Healdsburg	10/18	
Harvest Fair	Santa Rosa	10/4-5	
Junior Grand National Livestock Expo	San Francisco/ Daly City	4/6-18	20,000
Marin Co. Fair	San Rafael	6/29-7/4	76,292
Napa Co. Fair	Calistoga	7/3-8	40,074
Napa Town & Country Fair	Napa	8/1-5	86,735
Pumpkin Festival	Half Moon Bay	10/20-21	200,000
San Francisco Co. Fair & Flower Show	San Francisco	8/23-26	8,437
San Mateo Co. Fair	San Mateo	7/23-8/4	173,172
Santa Clara Co. Fair	San Jose	8/9-19	466,968
Solano Co. Fair	Vallejo	6/11-23	207,690
Sonoma Co. Fair	Santa Rosa	7/9-21	318,845
Sonoma-Marin Fair	Petaluma	6/27-7/1	60,699
Sonoma Valley Vintage Festival	Sonoma	9/15-16	15,000
Viticulture Show	Santa Rosa	8/22-23	
Walnut Festival	Walnut Creek	9/14-16	30,000

The Farmbelt as a Culture

With farmland goes a farming culture, an agricultural way of life. To sense its distinctiveness, you have only to open a local newspaper in Healdsburg or Dixon or Gilroy and skim the reports on crops and prices, the doings of the Future Farmers, the meetings of the 4-H Club.

The Bay Area has a tradition of farms and ranches owned by the families that run them. Many operations have been in the same families for generations. On such farms everybody, including the kids, is part of the crew. It may be hard to prove that this kind of upbringing makes a valuable citizen — a person both responsible and independent — but it has long been the fashion to think so. In rural towns where the family farm tradition is strong, people do seem to get involved easily in civic groups and community affairs: there are plenty of joiners.

Between two major parts of our region — the farmlands and the cities — a back-and-forth movement of people seems to occur. In one generation a ranch family may have no youngsters who want to continue on the land; but other young relatives, city-bred but exposed to farm life as children, step forward. The farmer's life, too rugged for most people most of the time, attracts a certain number of people at all times. There is value in keeping such an option open.

Art Rogers

These fairs have an honorable element of pure hype. (After the Pumpkin Festival began, pumpkin sales soared.) For the farmers, they are conventions of a sort: chances to trade information and moral support. For outsiders, they are entertainment first of all. But many urbanites who visit the fairs must go home impressed at the vigor of local agriculture, and sharply reminded of those natural rhythms on which life in the cities, no less than outside them, depends.

Sometimes farm festivals survive the agriculture that gave them their basis. Walnut Creek has hardly any walnut trees today, but its Walnut Festival carries on. There is something saddening about such a remnant when the old connection to the land is gone.

And that reminds us of the present danger. The connection between the Farmbelt and the city can be a rich and mutually profitable one. It *can be*. But those possibilities may disappear before we have the time to test them. In fact, unless we can change the direction of events, the metropolis may end by destroying the Farmbelt altogether.

Many farmers like living within easy reach of the great regional downtowns; isolation, a complaint still heard in purely rural regions, is hardly a problem here. Quite a few local farmers, in fact, live away from the farm; and quite a few combine farm work with other employment. In 1974, at least half of all Bay Area agriculturalists had some nonfarm income. This mixed style of life is another of the special options in our Farmbelt.

County fairs in the Bay Area draw over two million people a year. More specifically tied to agriculture are annual farm festivals. These go back to 1896 when the Sonoma Valley Vintage Festival began; the latest addition is the Gilroy Garlic Festival, now two years old. Sebastopol has its Apple Blossom Festival, Half Moon Bay its Pumpkin Festival, and so on.

FOCUS: The Green-Grocer's View

Joe Carcione is a man with a case to make. He used to be a wholesaler and exporter of produce; these days he's a full-time, syndicated, multimedia gadfly.

His number one target: growers who market green, tasteless, rubbery fruit, and vegetables that are less than fresh. His number two target: the public that fails to insist on something better.

In his small office upstairs at the produce terminal in South San Francisco, Carcione grows excited. "Sure, if you want to send fruit all the way to the East Coast, you've got to pick it green. But, by golly, people that live in a fruit-growing state are entitled to ripe and ready fruit. They are absolutely entitled to it!"

Most of the time, Carcione says, we don't get what's coming to us. He cites the examples everybody knows: the sugarless peaches; the rubber apricots; the starchy apples; the tomatoes turned red (but not ripe) by exposure to ethylene gas. "It's a sin. They say fresh fruit is the finest thing in the world for you. But is it? It isn't, if it isn't ripe. When you buy a peach without a peachy flavor, or an apricot without an apricoty flavor, you're getting it without nutrition."

Carcione, now in his sixties, has been in and around the produce business since 1932. He looks younger than he is: a short, square-faced man who speaks in a forceful, somewhat ragged

voice. It's a voice that radio and TV audiences know well. "I try to find out what's going on," he says. "I inform people when merchandise is high. I inform 'em when it's cheap. I inform 'em when it's at its best quality. I do these things."

What he hears from his public, in turn, encourages him. People *do* care about flavor, says Joe Carcione. They *do* care about nutritional value. And, he feels, it's in their power — *our* power — to demand better produce. "If the public insisted, the growers would respond."

And if people insisted, one group of growers at least would have a tremendous amount to gain: the farmers that operate close to Bay Area cities. They have, next door, a huge potential market for ripe-and-ready fruit. There is big money to be made, Carcione claims, in serving that market. Being close to the cities is one advantage; being small — most Bay Area operations are — is a second. On a small farm, it's easy to harvest carefully, picking fruit

at the right moment. "They shouldn't ever want to get too big," Carcione says.

How does the local grower reach the local public? There are ways. The simplest is direct marketing: the farmer announces his presence and lets the public come to him. It works. The State has a number — (800) 952-5272 — that people can call for announcements on where to go for produce. Whenever Joe gives that number on the air, "the response is tremendous. You can see that there's a need."

He has praise for some local growers who serve that need: the Crane Brothers in Penngrove in Sonoma County, for instance, and the Webb Ranch in Menlo Park. But what's happening now is the merest beginning. He points to the Brentwood area in eastern Contra Costa County. "They grow just about everything: peaches, apricots, figs, melons, tomatoes, squashes, corn. And if people knew

that they could go out there and buy at reasonable prices, those growers would sell all they could put out."

Then there are the farmers' markets, where producers bring their harvest to a central location. These are multiplying: two new ones, in Oakland and San Jose, opened up just last year, with Dixon and Redwood City joining the list this year.

Traditional markets, too, could serve local growers better if the farmers would seek them out. All over the region, specialized produce stores are opening up: stores that choose their stock with care and can answer the question: "What's good today?" Joe sees a future in which the small stores in the city will link to small farms in the country to bring in high-quality produce at competitive prices.

Even the biggest chain stores would favor local produce. "I don't care if you pick 10,000 boxes of tomatoes, you've got Safeway and Lucky and Alpha Beta to clean 'em up. These chains would be delighted to buy, because they would get a fresher product — a product that doesn't have to travel six or seven hundred miles."

The future then, looks promising. But Carcione has cautions for farmers. For direct marketed produce, part of the saving — the money that doesn't go to the middlemen — must be passed on to the consumer, and the quality of the produce must be kept high. "You have to put up a good pack."

"When you say locally grown produce," says Carcione, "you've got a psychological advantage. It means: riper. It means: sweeter. It means: fresher." That's the promise he'd like to see more Bay Area farmers — and consumers — take advantage of.

4 The Dwindling Farmbelt

Said the farmer watching the carpenters work next door: "They're doing their job and we've gotta do ours. I just hope there's a compromise somewhere in between."

So far in the Bay Area we have found no such compromise. When development and agriculture have competed for the same land, the farms and ranches, with few exceptions, have lost.

Bay Area Farmland Loss

Between 1949 and 1979, about 190,000 acres of Bay Area farmland went under buildings, asphalt and suburban lawns. Nearly all of this was in the broad flat valleys where building is easy and crops rich. Roughly a third of our total valley-floor cropland had disappeared by 1979.

Serious though it is, this kind of outright land coverage is just one component of a much more massive total loss. Not 190,000 but over 700,000 acres of agricultural land actually went out of production in these thirty years. What accounts for the rest of the loss?

A second portion of the missing farmland — at least 64,000 acres — is still unbuilt but lies idle, paralyzed, as it were, by the urban shadow. It is owned now by speculators, or by farmers who expect development so soon that farming seems not worth the effort. Yet another portion of the lost farmland — about 60,000 acres — is in parks, watershed lands, and other reserves that are closed to agricultural use. Since these special areas are there to serve the requirements of city people, their withdrawal from the Farmbelt must be considered a cost of urban growth. (It should be pointed out, however, that most of the remote parkland — 120,000 acres or more — remains agricultural: it is leased back to ranchers and farmers.)

But the largest single consumer of farmland — taking more land, apparently, than does outright subdivision — is the almost invisible process called parcelization: the breaking up of large rural properties into small ones. Though not as dramatic as the sea-of-houses type of urban expansion, this disintegration of farms is just as much a type of urbanization, and just as much a threat to the farm economy.

BAY AREA FARMLAND LOSS: 1949-1974

County	Cropland Change	Pasture and Range change*	Total Ag Land Change	Population Change (1950-74)	Acres Lost/ 100 Increase in Population
Alameda	− 48,550	+ 26,940	− 22,065	345,300	6.4
Contra Costa	− 70,885	+ 2,732	− 68,153	276,900	24.6
Marin	− 13,076	− 76,263	− 89,339	125,500	71.2
Napa**	− 31,510	− 63,505	− 95,015	41,600	228.4 (108 w/o Berryessa)
San Mateo	− 18,326	+ 16,836	− 1,490	333,900	.4
Santa Clara	−121,538	− 11,523	−133,106	860,700	15.5
Solano	+ 140	− 53,332	− 53,192	78,000	68.2
Sonoma	− 31,330	−101,179	−132,509	138,100	95.9
Bay Area	−335,575	−259,294	−594,869	2,200,000	27.0

*Apparent increases in rangeland are evidently partly the result of shifts between cropland and pasture, partly due to enumerating changes. They are not shown by Agricultural Commissioners' Reports.

**Lake Berryessa, approximately 50,000 acres.

Source: U.S. Bureau of the Census. *Censuses of Agriculture.* 1949-1974. California Department of Finance, Population Research Unit.

Small farms can be highly efficient. But most of these little properties don't wind up as producing farms at all; they finish as rural "estates," hobby farms, or "ranchettes." Aside from removing land from production directly, they create real difficulties for serious agriculture around them.

For one thing, they bring into the countryside people with urban habits and urban standards. Not surprisingly, the new settlers object to the dust, smells, and noises of the working farm — to say nothing of any pesticide use. And it works both ways: dogs harass livestock; trespassing youngsters leave gates open; property is vandalized and crops stolen. If ranchettes become numerous enough, the new rural homeowners may even band together and secure the passage of ordinances restricting what's done on adjacent farms.

Even when houses are not built, parcelization takes land off the agricultural market. The typical farm or ranch is not a single parcel but several — some owned, some typically leased. Operators commonly add parcels in a good year and may dispose of some in bad years. The small, expensive "ranchettes" are useless in this market may force a farmer to look far afield for suitable properties. Moreover, the example of their priciness tends to lift land prices around them.

Often parcelization has been the first step toward denser development. In other areas, ranchettes may be the ultimate use. The consequences for producing agriculture are the same in both cases.

Altogether, at least 177,000 acres of the total loss of Bay Area agricultural land — one fourth — has been due to parcel breakup. It's been happening fastest in and around Sebastopol and elsewhere in Sonoma County; in the Brentwood-Oakley area of east Contra Costa County; in the Tassajara Hills and elsewhere near the Livermore Valley; on the south San Mateo Coast; and around San Martin, south of Morgan Hill in the

Santa Clara Valley. The disintegration may be starting in west Marin and southern Sonoma County; in the Dry Creek Valley north of Santa Rosa; and in more remote parts of the Diablo Range south of Livermore.

There are a few other factors in the farmland loss. Some land has been physically ruined — by erosion, for instance, or by salt buildup in the soil. Some land — mostly the poorest — may have been abandoned simply because farming proved unprofitable there. But urban growth, with its effects, certainly accounts for two-thirds of the past loss, and probably more than that. This proportion can be expected to increase dramatically.

How does this process look from the point of view of the people in the middle — the farmers and ranchers themselves?

They find themselves in a difficult situation. Most of them do want to keep on farming; yet as cities reach out toward them, they find it harder to do their work and harder to ignore the temptation that high land prices pose.

The plain truth is that farmland — no matter how rich, no matter how irreplaceable — sells at higher prices for residential use than it does for continued agriculture. No sensible owner can be expected to ignore this fact.

When an agricultural district begins to disintegrate, an attitude sets in that hurries the process along. People tell each other that the end is inevitable. "You hear that often enough," says one dairy owner, "and you almost feel like packing your bags and sitting on the front porch." Not surprisingly, some owners stop pouring in the money and labor that a long haul farming operation requires.

Meanwhile, pressure is mounting. Land prices climb clear out of a farmer's reach. New residents arrive, and small, annoying conflicts between farmers and homeowners set in. As more and more farms shut down, a partial collapse of

FOCUS: The Next Five San Joses?

RAPID GROWTH AREAS

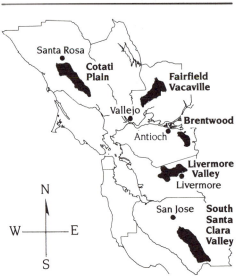

The Santa Clara Valley case is not unique. What happened there can happen again — and by the signs, it's about to.

During the last three decades, the growing population of the region has mostly been housed on the great Bay Plain: the lowland that circles San Francisco Bay from San Bruno to San Jose and north again to Richmond. Today this easily-developed rim is all but completely built over. Already the pressure is shifting outward to new targets: new valley lands, not so different from the northern Santa Clara Valley as it once was.

Which of these will be the next San Jose?

essential agricultural services can further accelerate the loss. The healthy north bay dairy industry, for instance, has its center at Petaluma, where many competing merchants sell fodder and supplies. But if the number of dairies were to drop too far, some of these services would disappear; others would become high-priced monopolies.

The Santa Clara Valley had 200 packing plants in 1959; today there are only a handful, and these have much more capacity than local farmers can fill. The packers import raw products from outside the Valley. But if Santa Clara's own farmland continues to dwindle, the plants may lose their last reason for staying where they are.

When a piece of the Farmbelt dies, the process is almost like the death of a living thing: everything goes wrong at once.

There's nothing unique about all this. Special as the Bay Area's agricultural land is, the process by which we lose it is exactly the one going on around San Diego or Santa Barbara or, for that matter, around Boston. It is anonymous. That is part of what makes it painful.

Southern Santa Clara Valley. Just south of the present urban front lies the Coyote Valley, with 3,500 acres of prime soil; 40 percent of that land is within San Jose city limits, but the City has decided to halt growth at the Coyote Narrows — for now. However, the City did permit IBM to build a plant in the threatened area three years ago, and more recently to expand it.

Farther south, the town of Morgan Hill has set a yearly limit on building (but has an industrial park in mind for the north edge of town). The next center, Gilroy, plans to convert acres of cropland to housing and industry. Parcel breakup, meanwhile, is happening up and down the long valley, with hotspots north of Morgan Hill and north of Gilroy at San Martin.

If San Jose continues its present growth patterns, a county study indicates, it will run out of land to develop north of the Coyote Narrows by 1990. It is then that the pressure on the South Valley will really begin.

The Livermore Valley. Compact and separate, the cities of Pleasanton and Livermore may not stay that way for long. Their projected final boundaries would cover 80 percent of the valley floor. A proposed Las Positas "New Town" — submitted to the voters twice in the 1970's and twice rejected — is still a going proposal; it would fill 4,300 acres north of Livermore, Along the north rim of the basin, in the fertile, rolling

Farmland Loss:
A Coming National Crisis?

Every year, in the United States, we lose not less than three million acres of cropland.

A few years ago it was possible to wonder how much this mattered. There seemed to be plenty of land: land inexhaustible. But now that world is gone forever. We are rapidly reaching the point where *no* agricultural land is expendable. Here's why.

The world *demand* for food grows steadily with population. So does the more specific demand for luxury items like grain-fed beef: the foodstuffs many American farmers have made their specialty. (For better or for worse, people in countries of increasing affluence are imitating the American diet.) In 1968, one out of five American farm acres served the export market; now the proportion is two out of five. As the Russian grain sales of the early 1970's proved, foreign demand can drive prices at home sharply upward.

Meanwhile, *per-acre yields* are no longer reliably increasing. Without ever quite realizing it, we have lived through an extraordinary 20-year boom period in which each year could be counted on to bring more harvest from each acre tilled. Since the late 60's, however, the

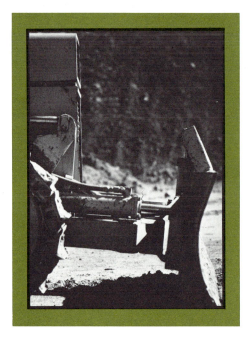

Tassajara Hills, five and twenty-acre ranchettes are being chopped out wholesale. Population growth in the valley is hefty now — some 2 percent a year — and is expected to accelerate.

Fairfield. Growth came late to this area along the San Francisco-Sacramento corridor, but is proceeding quickly. Fairfield plans to channel development southwest along Interstate 80 toward Cordelia; Vallejo is pushing northeast, also toward Cordelia. Vacaville, by contrast, is making a serious attempt to manage its growth. Right now, the Solano County corridor is the fastest-growing portion of the Bay Area; more close-in agricultural land is slated for development here than in any other county.

increases have been erratic. And each new increment is costing us more in energy, money, pollution, and erosion. Added to this are climate uncertainties. Many believe that we are due for a swing to a colder climate, cutting yields from more northerly croplands.

If demand is growing and per-acre yields are not, only one thing can maintain the balance: the planting of more land. Whether we look at the world scene from a humanitarian viewpoint or from a self-interested one — in terms of balance of trade and prices — one fact is clear: abundant farmland is an asset no nation, not even ours, can afford to squander.

We need to protect not only land being farmed today, but also land that might have to be called upon in the future — or more immediately, in case of a transient crisis. Thus, in 1972, crop failures overseas caused American farmers to plow acreage that had long lain fallow. Later, foreign demand dropped back, and the marginal land was retired again. But the need to "call up the reserves" raised the serious question: just how big *are* those reserves?

In 1975, the United States had an estimated 413 million acres of planted cropland. Another 127 million acres had

---

Brentwood. The rich plains of East Contra Costa south of the Delta are no longer free of pressure. Neighboring areas — Pittsburg and Antioch — have just about used up their flat land. If Walnut Creek and Concord become employment centers, Brentwood could boom. It's prepared to: the city's general plan would triple the urban area by the year 2000. The County forsees low-density growth in the surrounding area. Already the fringes of town are checker-boarded with five and ten-acre parcels — often too small for raising of the fruits and vegetables for which the area is known.

The Cotati Plain. It's a northern counterpart of the Santa Clara Valley: 30,000 acres of fertile ground from Petaluma north to Healdsburg. Rohnert Park is the present hotspot for growth; it is already linking up with Santa Rosa, and only a narrow unprotected greenbelt divides these towns from Sebastopol, the North Bay apple capital. Piecemeal growth at Windsor threatens the agricultural strip between Santa Rosa and Healdsburg (though local voters recently turned down a plan to make Windsor a city with sprawling boundaries). Parcelization, meanwhile, is rapid near Sebastopol and north of Healdsburg in the vineyards of the Dry Creek Valley.

Barry Rokeach

"high or medium potential" for planting: the fallow reserve. But that figure far exaggerates the cushion. Most of the fallow land is markedly inferior to land now under the plow. Only a portion could be brought into production without elaborate preparation. This relatively amenable land — the "ready reserve" — amounted to no more than 35 million acres, and possibly less than 25 million.

If even that seems like a lot of countryside, set it against the basic loss statistic: the one million acres of U.S. land that goes out of business each year. If the lost land is replaced with land from the ready reserve, that reserve will drop to nothing in two decades. All at once we will find ourselves at the end of the cropland frontier — the era when land, like oil a few years ago, seemed not to matter.

Much of this information has only recently become widely known. It has already produced the first signs of a crisis mood. If the loss is not halted, says Agriculture Secretary Bob Bergland, we are on "a collision course with disaster. I don't know when it's going to stop," he adds, "but stop it must." The private American Land Forum warns: "When the problem does 'go critical,' it may be beyond remedy." A major National Agricultural Lands Study is underway. Bills to set national policy have begun to appear in Congress. Many states — Oregon, Washington, Iowa, Wisconsin, Connecticut, Massachusetts — have taken some action (not always effective) to safeguard farmland. This time it's California — the greatest farm state of them all — that is lagging conspicuously behind.

Taken alone, the Bay Area's Farmbelt is a tiny part of the nation's stock of agricultural land; and what we lose here is a tiny part of what the nation annually loses. But then the same thing is true of *any* region. The problem is everywhere; it has no center. No area that has significant farmland left is excused from the task of doing something to save it.

At least half of the farmland lost in the U.S. each year — and probably more — is lost by conversion to urban uses. Conversion happens through thousands of decisions, made by thousands of local governments. In Novato or Fairfield, Morgan Hill or Brentwood, it may be hard to see how one's local decision affecting farmland can matter. But matter it does.

If the national problem is to be dealt with at all, it must be dealt with in the hundred situations like ours: in the regions where, acre by acre, cities and city influences press out upon the farms.

Fighting Back:
What Local Government is Doing

QUESTION: Isn't anything being done
to protect Bay Area farmland?
ANSWER: Yes, quite a bit.
QUESTION: Is it helping?
ANSWER: Not much.

Though many agencies of government have some influence over what happens to farmland, the job of deciding land-use remains essentially with the counties and cities. Since the late 1960's, many of these governments have adopted — at least on paper — the idea that farmland should be preserved. Few, however, have gone beyond policy to action; and even with the best intentions, progress has been uncertain.

The Cities

Several Bay Area cities have substantial amounts of farmland within their present city limits that they intend to develop. (Cities that may decide to maintain some islands of agriculture are Morgan Hill, Fremont, Half Moon Bay, and Petaluma.)

More significant are plans for future annexations. Today cities try to avoid disorderly "leapfrog" growth: the urban front is to move out steadily. But it is to move indefinitely. Only one city — Novato — has yet proposed to set a future boundary that renounces development of nearby farmland. (Growth control ordinances in several cities — Petaluma, Morgan Hill, Vacaville, Sonoma do have the incidental effect of postponing pressure on surrounding agriculture.)

The expansion of cities is regulated by bodies — one in each county — called Local Agency Formation Commissions. Made up mainly of local government officials, they assign to each city a

"sphere of influence" or probable ultimate boundary. "Spheres of influence" are usually drawn broadly, and they are rarely designed to avoid farmland.

The Counties

Most of the Farmbelt, by its nature, is still outside city limits: unincorporated areas where county government regulates land use. But county general plans, while lately eloquent about open space, seldom contain much solid policy on agricultural land. When subdivisions and development questions come before Planning Commissions and Boards of Supervisors, the fate of farmland is rarely the issue it ought to be. Some counties are exceptions, and in several counties the picture is improving. But in too many cases, strong policies have not yet been clearly established.

In dealing with agricultural land, counties have three major tools available: exclusive zoning for agriculture; large lot-size requirements to inhibit subdivision; and the Williamson Act tax reduction program.

The first — zoning exclusively for agriculture — is the most direct and powerful method. It is not, unfortunately, in use in the Bay Area. Such a zone is comparable to areas set aside exclusively for industry: it precludes any use in a farmland area that is in conflict with agriculture. Something of this sort has been applied in Oregon. California local governments have been slow to take advantage of this tool. This leaves them with the remaining two methods — indirect and cumbersome approaches to the problem.

The second method — controlling parcel size — is widely used. A county will impose a minimum size below which ownerships in rural areas cannot be split. On each such minimum parcel, just one house or "dwelling unit" is allowed. Current ordinances set minimum size as low as five acres (in Contra Costa County) and as high as 160 acres (in parts of Napa, Solano, and Santa Clara Counties).

These large-lot districts — sometimes labeled agricultural zones — really don't function as such. Because of the one house permitted on each parcel,

they allow ranches to be carved up into non-productive rural estates. In western Marin, where a sixty-acre requirement prevails, buyers have appeared who are happy to purchase that much land as a personal back yard. In Alameda County, 100-acre homesites have been carved out on a number of occasions.

Large-lot zoning can be a useful partial tool, provided that the minimum parcel size is set large enough. The need is for parcels to stay large enough to be attractive for purchase or lease *by farmers*. From crop to crop this threshold size varies — any single minimum size is arbitrary. But much of the land in question is hilly ranching country, and pieces smaller that about 100 acres are rarely of interest to ranchers. A special Farmlands Project study reached the disquieting conclusion that only the 160-acre zone, the largest yet applied in the Bay Area, comes close to retaining the necessary minimum for grazing.

If every accessible parcel of rural land in the Bay Area were split down to the size allowed by ordinance, it would be, for agriculture, a disaster. Commercial cattle ranching would virtually disappear, and crop production, too, would be very much hampered.

The third tool is the Williamson Act. Under this 1965 law, California farmers may sign agreements with local governments by which they agree to keep farming for ten years. Unless either party gives notice, the contract renews itself each year. In return, property taxes are cut. Though reduced in importance by the passage of Proposition 13, this tax break is definitely still attractive. Williamson Act contracts cover 70% of the Bay Area's grazing land and 30% of its cropland.

The Williamson Act has helped farmers and brought fairer taxation to a lot of farmland. How much it has helped to slow farmland loss is another question. It requires only a ten-year commitment; and landowners who might have been tempted to sell or develop within a decade have often avoided Williamson Act contracts.

The Act can be more useful if a county chooses to regulate land under contract more strictly than uncontracted land. Napa and Marin seem to be making this connection. They do not automatically permit Williamson Act owners to split their land down to the minimum parcel sizes. Other counties,

though they may set higher minimum sizes for Williamson Act land, don't object to parcel splits. In some cases, cancellation of a contract (without the ten-year waiting period) has been allowed for the flimsiest of reasons — simply to allow for immediate development. Thus used, the act is hardly better than no program at all.

The Problem of Uncertainty

Local action to stop farmland loss is difficult for several reasons:

★ Local officials tend to underestimate the effect of "minor" exceptions to good rules: rezonings and variances, a lot-split here, the cancellation of a Williamson Act contract there. Made one after another, a series of such exceptions can amount to a major land-use change.

★ City councils and boards of supervisors have been shifting viewpoints with bewildering rapidity. One election creates at 3-2 majority in favor of retaining farmland, the next may destroy it. Continuous policy is hard to come by.

★ To add still more uncertainty, city limits move outward by annexation; the land-use discouraged by the county in one month may be endorsed by a city government in the next.

Three votes, and a thirty-day waiting period, suffice to change a zoning ordinance. And each time a decision is made against retaining farmland, losses occur that can never be repaired. It adds up to what has been termed "a tyranny of small decisions," taking the region steadily in a direction its people no longer want to go.

ABAG

In 1970, the Association of Bay Area Governments — the voluntary regional council of cities and counties — approved a regional plan that called for a very different future. ABAG proposed that the next twenty years of urban growth be kept close to the existing cities. Outside those areas marked for growth, it proposed a 3.4 million acre system of protected open space. Though saving farmland was not the primary goal of this plan, much farmland would have been protected under it — had it ever been carried out. Unfortunately, neither ABAG nor its plans have real authority.

The widely admired proposal has not yet been acted upon. And the organization's recent projections of growth and growth patterns acknowledge that obvious fact: plan or no plan, business goes on as usual.

Action From Sacramento

Two state programs aim at protecting farmland. The first is the Williamson Act tax-break system described above. The second is the coastal planning program established in 1976. The California Coastal Commission has a clear mandate to protect agricultural land. Under the eye of the Coastal Commission and

FOCUS: What The Counties Are Doing

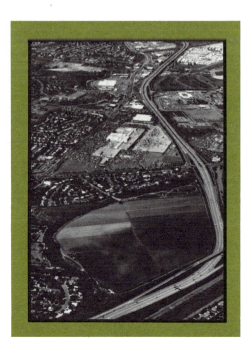

San Mateo....The County's open space plan says little about farmland. A "resource management zone" is applied in rural areas; it allows development on five-to-forty acre parcels. Because much of San Mateo's farmland is in the coastal zone, state law now requires the County to develop strong farmland protection plans.

Marin....In 1972 Marin County adopted a pioneering general plan that, among other things, reversed a long-standing county policy of allowing development in the western dairylands. Minimum lot size in most rural areas today is 60 acres; parcels under Williamson Act contracts can not be split at all. Though the plan says less

its subordinate regional commissions, local governments along the coast are now writing Local Coastal Plans; these too must include farmland protection. But generally the area covered is only a narrow seaside strip. There is also a Coastal Conservancy, with authority to buy interests in coastal farmland — but without much of a budget to do it with.

Though the Legislature has recognized farmland loss as a serious problem statewide, no new actions are to be expected soon. Farmland protection measures were debated in 1977 and 1978, and significant bills twice passed the Assembly. After the passage of Proposition 13, though, the Legislature became much more cautious about any major new programs.

Had one of the bills been enacted, local governments statewide would have been required to map out "farmland reserves" according to guidelines set in the law. But the bills, drafted to avoid the objections of local governments, came equipped with multiple exceptions that would have limited their usefulness where farms and cities mix. In the Bay Area, they would have missed much critical land in Santa Clara County, east Contra Costa County, and elsewhere. They would not have touched the largest component of the Farmbelt, the

than it might about agriculture as such, this county — more than any other in the Bay Area — has made it a habit to support local agriculture. An unusual coalition of ranchers and conservationists has helped make the new policy work. A major problem, however, is the permitted lot size: 60 acres is too small for the agricultural land market and well within the reach of the buyers of "ranchettes." Some ranches have splintered into minimum parcels, and land prices are being driven up. To counter the trend, ranchers themselves (with the help of other local citizens) have set up an Agricultural Land Trust in partnership with the County. Its major strategy: to work out arrangements by which farmland owners forego development permanently in exchange for tax benefits.

Napa.... Napa was the first Bay Area county to take strong action on farmland. In 1968, it classified its vineyard-covered central valley as an "agricultural preserve." Minimum parcel size in the valley was recently increased to 40 acres, and the Williamson Act is well-used here. County policy has been less effective in regard to grazing lands, especially to the south. In some areas (where fire hazard exists) a 160-acre zone prevails; elsewhere, lots may be split to 40 acres. A recent change in the Board of Supervisors may weaken some of the County's pioneering measures. The expansion plans of the town of American Canyon near Vallejo are an added threat.

superlative rangelands. And they would not have dealt with the problem of parcelization.

Then there is Governor Brown's Urban Strategy. It calls for an end to urban sprawl and proposes a number of important measures toward that goal. The Legislature has enacted some of these but so far has required no specific action by local governments. While the Strategy does state the importance of protecting farmland, its focus is elsewhere. No separate strategy on agricultural land is yet in the works.

There is, in sum, no reason to expect Sacramento to take this problem off our hands. And while state action to preserve farmland is still something to hope for, a statewide law out of Sacramento could hardly be tailored to fit local conditions exactly. It could be a valuable aid, but no more.

Sonoma.... Farmland has only recently become an issue in Sonoma County. In the past, the county has had permissive rural zoning, usually with ten and twenty acre lot-size minimums, rural subdivisions were allowed to mingle with commercial agriculture. The situation may now improve: a major county study recently acknowledged that the zoning "is not adequate for preserving agricultural land": zoning changes are being proposed; and the Sonoma County Farm Bureau has presented a plan for special "agricultural production zones." On the minus side, growth pressures are strong, and recent changes in the Board of Supervisors may make action difficult. Meanwhile, cities within the county — notably Rohnert Park and Santa Rosa — plan much more expansion into farming areas.

Solano.... In 1976, the County applied 80- and 160-acre minimum parcel sizes to most of the county's cropland and rangeland. This strong commitment has not stopped Solano from approving a number of rural estate subdivisions in the northwest part of the county, however. More threatening — and not under County control — is the expansion of the cities: Vallejo, Benicia, Fairfield, and Vacaville. Says one county official, looking at development plans: "We're just nibbling away at agriculture."

Contra Costa.... This county has no significant policies for farmland protection. Its general plan has little to say on the issue, and in its "agricultural" zones the County applies five and twenty-acre minimum lot sizes — too small for the area's serious farming and ranching land market. Rural estate divisions are widespread in the Tassajara hills and the East County near Brentwood,

The View from Washington

Still less likely is help from Washington — assuming even that such help would be a good thing. Though concern is mounting, the federal government has as yet no real policy on saving farmland. Bills on the subject have begun to appear in Congress, but all have died.

There are two kinds of action the federal government may eventually take. The first might be a program of grants to local governments that try to protect farmland. The second would be an attempt to police federal actions for their effect on farmland. Thousands of federal programs — from home loans to energy development, from transportation to defense — help determine what happens to agricultural land. More often than not, the weight of federal action falls on the side of farmland loss. Simply to correct this pattern would be a powerful step.

Most unlikely is any federal attempt to intervene in local land-use decisions, even if this could legally be done.

---

the last remaining agricultural areas. In the same areas, major development is being anticipated, and speculators have made large purchases of land. Low density suburban growth accounts for most of the farmland loss in Contra Costa; County as well as city policies still actively encourage this type of sprawl.

Alameda.... In 1972, the county took a bold step and established a 100-acre parcel size for its farming and grazing area. Until 1977, this zone prevented ranch breakup, but in that year several large properties were broken into 100-acre estates. For the last two years an informal moratorium has prevailed, but the zoning itself has not been modified. Depending on the balance of opinion on the Board of Supervisors, the way toward wholesale parcelization may be open. There is pressure also for urban development in the Livermore Valley and adjacent foothills.

Santa Clara.... Beginning with the "greenbelt zone" in 1958, the County has tried several times to protect agricultural land. More recently, in a bitterly controversial action, the County increased the minimum parcel size in agricultural areas from 2.5 to 20, 40, and — in remote mountain country — 160 acres. Today, the County is pushing toward adoption of a new general plan, and will probably approve its first effective pro-farmland policies late in 1980. These will improve protection, but will not limit the expansion of cities and some rural communities. "These policies are the best we can do right now," one Santa Clara official says, "but I'm concerned about the future."

Prospect: A Steepening Slide

In thirty years, three quarters of a million acres gone. If that huge figure were just a historical quirk, a one-time tradeoff of Bay Area farms for cities, there would be cause for regret, perhaps, but no real cause for alarm.

But the truth is that the rate of farmland loss in the region is not decreasing. Not a bit. In fact, there are indications that the process is moving much faster now than before.

Between 1949 and 1974, farmland went out of production at an average rate of 19,000 acres a year. But the average conceals an increasing rate. In the early 1970's — the last period for which complete information is available — loss was proceeding at *four times* the average pace. That was just before energy prices soared; high transportation costs should theoretically encourage tighter development patterns. That effect, however, is not yet visible. In outlying suburbs we are still putting four to six houses on an acre (the regional average is eight to the acre). Still farther out, in rural areas, the boom in country estates of five to twenty acres continues; a whole ranch may go out of production to create just a handful of homesites. In the past we've lost level cropland faster than hilly rangeland. This proportion appears to be reversing as development climbs the hills and "ranchettes" become a more widespread use of land.

On the basis of growth projections county by county, we seem due to lose in the next fifteen years not less than 375,000 more acres of Bay Area crop and

BAY AREA FARMLAND LOSS

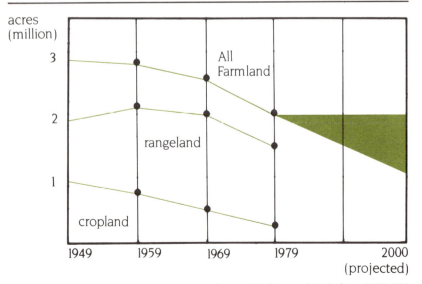

Source: U.S. Census of Agriculture (1974) POS Farmlands Project estimates

rangeland — 20% of the Farmbelt of today. In fact, this is an optimistic guess: it represents the slower long-term rate, not the faster recent rate of loss.

Unless we act, the question is not whether we will lose the Farmbelt: the question is only when. If the postwar clip of conversion holds steady, we will shut down every farm and ranch in the region in less than a hundred years. And if losses pick up speed, as seems only too likely, the virtual end of the Farmbelt will come much sooner: within the lifetimes of many who read this report.

Unless we act, we can see ahead, not the sensational nightmare of a San Jose covering all nine counties, but a future hardly more desirable: the fertile flatlands covered almost totally with housing; the hillsides partly developed and partly fallow, with vast areas carved up into ranchettes and expansive rural estates. There would still be scenery in such a future; there would still be considerable "open space," but from the land of the Bay Area would come no food. The farm economy, the living fabric that is Bay Area agriculture, would be gone.

The head of one county's Farm Bureau puts it well. "I'm not an alarmist," he says, "but the time to start doing something has arrived."

5 The Permanent Farmbelt

And there you have it. The farmland of the Bay Area is a precious resource; it is also on the road to extinction. The next two decades of growth may well erode the Farmbelt so deeply and in so many places that our chance to preserve it as a living whole, as a major part of the region's life, will disappear. The time to act is not tomorrow, when our farmland capital is still further diminished: it is today.

Neither the state nor the federal government is likely to step in with a sweeping program to halt the impending losses. That is probably just as well. Judging by past performance, programs devised in Sacramento or Washington are unlikely to fit local needs. And the Bay Region has a history of ingenuity in meeting challenges like this one without prompting from higher levels of government.

It seems equally unpromising to wait for our *current* local policies to take stronger hold. Though many local governments are trying hard — though some have made progress toward stemming farmland loss — their combined efforts fall far short of success. That is probably to be expected. The Farmbelt is regional. The benefits it gives us accrue to the whole Bay Area, and the process of its loss is regionwide as well. Local governments simply cannot deal with a problem of this scale.

What is left, then, is the need for a nine-county approach, an exercise in regional home rule.

Regional Action: A Bay Area Tradition

More than most regions, the Bay Area recognizes itself as a single extended community. We have also a strong tradition of deciding issues by local vote. Sometimes the two elements combine: the public is asked to give its verdict on questions that cross county lines.

★ In 1962, voters in three counties were asked to tax themselves for a proposed mass transit system, BART. (They agreed.)

★ In 1972, the people of three counties went to the polls to decide whether a second Bay Bridge, the controversial Southern Crossing, should be built. (They said no.)

Richard Conrat/BCDC

★ Two subregional park and open space districts — East Bay in 1934 and Midpeninsula in 1972 — have been created by popular vote. (Several Bay counties have also voted to tax themselves specially to purchase open space.)

★ The Save the Bay campaign of the 1960's produced the highly effective Bay Conservation and Development Commission (BCDC), responsible for Bay preservation and control of shoreline development in all nine counties. The approval of BCDC by the Legislature was a major accomplishment of area-wide citizen action.

★ We have long had nine-county regional agencies for air and water pollution control. We also have an areawide transportation agency — the Metropolitan Transportation Commission — and the voluntary Association of Bay Area Governments (ABAG). ABAG has prepared nine-county plans on many subjects; its Regional Plan of 1970 was the first general plan for the Bay Area. However, the agency lacks power: its plans can only focus desirable goals.

Lessons From Elsewhere

And how have other areas dealt with the farmland loss problem?

The simplest and most sweeping program is the one established in 1972 in British Columbia. A special agency of the provincial government controls the use of all farmland parcels larger than two acres outside city boundaries. Grazing land is included. In the Agricultural Land Reserves, as they are called, land-use changes that would damage agriculture are simply not permitted. Later subsidies for agriculture have gradually won farmers' support for these regulations.

Oregon's program is more complex. Under the 1972 Oregon law, all local governments must prepare plans that carry out state-established goals. One of those goals is the preservation of productive agricultural land, defined as that in soil classes I-IV and in some areas, I-VI. A state agency — the Land Conservation and Development Commission — interprets the goals and reviews local plans for compliance. Until plans are certified, the Commission itself hears appeals on local development issues.

Several American states — notably New York, Wisconsin, and Hawaii — have special plans or zoning districts designed to protect farmland. However, (except in Hawaii) these programs are essentially voluntary: owners must sign up to be included. Nor do they take aim at the central problem: the disappearance of farmland at the fringe of the metropolis.

Needed: A Commission, A Plan, A Vote

We do not recommend the hasty choice of any single method as the final "right answer" for Bay Area farmland preservation. A change in our land-use regulation methods is not, after all, something to be undertaken lightly. It requires deliberation and debate. At the same time, the erosion of the Farmbelt must be swiftly controlled.

To meet the claims both of haste and of caution, we propose a three-step process. A temporary Agricultural Land Commission should be established by the Legislature; it should prepare a detailed plan for agricultural preservation; and that plan should be submitted to the nine-county public for a verdict at the polls.

The Bay Area Agricultural Land Commission would have a limited lifetime (perhaps two to three years) and a clear assignment. There would be three key jobs for it to do:

1. to define the public interest in the Farmbelt and work out a means of protecting that interest.
2. to study the Bay Area's agriculture — its nature, its values, its needs — and to present this information in forms the public can use.
3. to protect the Farmbelt from encroachment during the study period.

To perform this last task, the Commission would need the authority to review local government actions that threaten the Farmbelt.

There are, of course, alternatives. For instance, the Legislature might simply require local governments to provide for farmland protection in local policies and plans. But even this mandate, to have any real effect, would require some sort of overall agency to review the resulting actions.

Another option: the Agricultural Lands Commission could be set up as a permanent body from the start. But this would not allow time for public debate and the resulting sorting-out of issues. It would leave the people of the region out of this huge decision. And who else should decide the future of the Bay Area's irreplaceable Farmbelt?

The Agricultural Land Commission

Even the interim commission would require careful design. The debate in the Legislature would undoubtedly yield some good ideas for making the body effective: exactly the purpose of such proceedings. The details could vary. Certain principles, however, should be kept in mind.

• *The Commission's goals must be well-defined.* It should concern itself with agricultural land, not with the broader issue of open space. Its aims should be to work out protective measures capable of application to all or most of the Bay Area's productive agricultural land. The importance of agriculture should be recognized in the legislative charge.

• *The Commission's jurisdiction must be broad.* It should concern itself with all cropland and grazing land in the region. To focus only on cultivated land, or on "prime" land, would be to ignore the complex interrelationships that hold the Farmbelt together. Much land, of course, would be quite properly excluded: all built-up areas, public lands, and forested areas. The interim Commission's jurisdiction — however defined — should not be considered the limit of whatever action the Commission might propose for the future.

• *The Commission must be able to protect the land it studies.* Pending the decisive popular vote, the agency should have authority to hold the Farmbelt intact. This means veto power over any conversion of farmland and ranchland into non-productive real estate — whether by subdivision or by parcelization. Such power could rest solely with the Commission, or it could be shared with local governments. Either way, the restrictions are bound to cause sharp debate. Disagreement will test all arguments and will help the Commission

Richard Conrat/BCDC

produce a realistic plan. The body should have no power to regulate actual farming practices, nor should the construction of buildings for agriculture be subject to Commission review.

• *The Commission must explore ways of supporting agriculture.* Merely preserving farmland may not be enough. The Commission should prepare a proposal to help Bay Area agriculturalists deal with other problems they face, including financial ones.

• *The Commission's work must be done in the open.* It must solicit the ideas of local governments, farmers and ranchers, competent experts on agricultural matters, and people at large. The more media coverage, the better. Everything possible should be done to inform the public of, and involve them in these important decisions.

The Plan and the Election

Just what the interim Commission might propose is, of course, not predictable. It is possible that it would recommend a permanent agency very much like itself. This is the route by which the Bay Commission was established, except that BCDC got its final charter from the Legislature. We believe

that any permanent Bay Area Agricultural Land Commission should be created only by voters of the region themselves.

If the agency continues, it could take several forms. It might retain direct control of development decisions on agricultural land; or it might assign the job to local governments, reserving the power to review and overrule in controversial cases.

We have good examples of both systems here in the Bay Area. Around the shoreline of San Francisco Bay proper, the Bay Commission has direct authority over filling and other proposals that would alter the Bay. But in 1977, when the Commission's jurisdiction was extended to cover the upland areas around Suisun Marsh as well, a different method was selected. After BCDC developed an initial preservation plan, the local governments of Solano County were charged with carrying it out. Now the County and several cities are primarily responsible for the 85,000-acre marsh; BCDC remains in the background to hear appeals in specific cases.

71

When the Agricultural Land Commission has prepared its plan, it will be time to place its recommendation before the people of the nine Bay counties for approval or rejection. Thus, for the first time, the fate of the Farmbelt will be a thing that each of us can help decide. And only thus can it be certain that any plan adopted expresses the public will.

Support For Agriculture

Preserving the land itself is the first step in securing the future of Bay Area agriculture, but it is not the last. Land loss, the greatest danger to the Farmbelt, is not the only threat.

The Farmlands Project spent much of its time surveying and analyzing the other problems facing ranchers and farmers. It concluded that, except for speculative land prices, local agriculture is essentially healthy — but that, to do well, it will need some increased support from the metropolis it serves in so many ways:

1. How can the region's small farmers be helped to market their products more competitively?
2. How can they better exploit the large local market for fresh produce?
3. How can we help beginning farmers and ranchers acquire land?
4. How can inheritance taxes be made less of a burden?
5. How can long-term credit be provided to finance improvements and purchase of land?
6. How can local ordinances that hamper farm operations be reformed?
7. What can be done to counter trespassing and vandalism?
8. How can the people of the region be made aware of their stake in the health of the region's agriculture?

A strategy for keeping agriculture alive in the Bay Area must include answers to these questions. Yet the first and overriding challenge is to make sure that the land, itself, remains.

The Challenge

That the people of the Bay Area want agricultural land preserved is beyond doubt. Local governments agree; their plans and policy statements almost always call (in highly general terms) for the protection of farmland. But the Farmbelt dwindles all the while.

What's lacking is a mechanism to carry out the public will. We can end this helplessness. We should do so now.

What is here proposed may seem drastic to many. Others, on the contrary, may find it not strong enough. To all we say: tell us how better to safeguard the region's farmland. Show us a better way — *but show us a way*.

The nine-county Bay Area has a reputation for solving knotty problems. We have perhaps the best park system of any major metropolitan center in this country. We took hold of water and air pollution problems sooner and more effectively than most comparable urban regions. In an era when federal funds went only to highways, we financed and built the first new rapid transit system in America in modern times. We have halted and even reversed the shrinkage of the open water and wetlands of our Bay.

These accomplishments can be seen as partial, sometimes fumbling, responses to a single vast imperative: the need to establish, between the metropolis we live in and the natural systems that support it, a sounder and more stable relationship. We are attempting, one might say, to replace a situation analogous to war with something like a negotiated peace.

The task of saving the Farmbelt is only a part of that large undertaking. But it is a tougher issue than any yet brought to the table. To resolve it will require all our craft and all our best good will.

That is the farmland challenge.

Art Rogers

A Future With Farms

Imagine, if you will, the Bay Area twenty years after its citizens have acted to save the region's Farmbelt:

*The many benefits of the Farmbelt already described will be guaranteed, enhanced or established anew: "buy local" campaigns will be sponsored by County Farm Bureaus and public agencies, as people start noticing just where their produce comes from and stores respond. Wastewater from our cities will irrigate more of our fields. From its small beginnings, direct marketing of goods from farmer to consumer will vastly expand. As time goes on, more sophisticated types of direct marketing will appear. Growers will band in cooperatives, and will establish links with similar associations of neighborhood stores and with larger retailers. More than ever, the Farmbelt will be a tourist attraction — the travel industry will bill it as such. Schools and civic organizations will greatly expand educational programs about local farmland.

*For the farmers, the assurance of a *permanent* Farmbelt will bring more concentration on making the land — and their business — produce. Initial dismay by some over loss of a possible development windfall will be replaced by a growing satisfaction, a demand that agriculture be given acknowledgement and support as the Bay Area's "special" industry. The public and local governments will grow to respect and support this claim. Together, farmers and the public will find ways to assist agriculture in times of trouble (as in Marin during the 1976-77 drought).

*For the cities, a permanent Farmbelt will help create a limit to outward sprawl, and will redirect energies toward making neighborhoods and downtowns livable, energy-efficient and joyous places to be.

*The Bay Area itself will be known and respected for its early action in meeting the farmland crisis. Our contribution will be the nation's gain — we will show that it is possible for a major metropolis to slow the destructive rate of national farmland loss.

The Farmbelt preserved will be the Farmbelt redicovered: a resource we value doubly because we recognized it in time. We will learn from it, admire it, and defend it. It will be a landmark in people's mind — an object, like the Bay, of local patriotism.

We will come to regard it as an inheritance, precious and inalienable.

The POS Farmlands Project

The POS Farmlands Project was a two-year study of the Bay Area's agricultural land. The work of the project was organized to respond to the following key questions:
1. What is agriculture in the nine-county Bay Area?
2. What are the functions of the region's farmlands?
3. What are the main issues facing agriculture in the region?
4. What will happen to Bay Area farmland if trends continue?
5. What farmlands should be protected and how should that be done?
6. How should farmlands preservation relate to urban development in the Bay Area?

The research program for the project was centered around a series of six background reports, one on each of the above questions. For several reports, special technical memos were prepared. In addition, there were four special studies undertaken on topics of specific interest. All of these reports are available from POS for the prices noted:

BACKGROUND REPORTS
1. Farmland and Farming in the Bay Area. A Description ($4.00)
2. The Functions of the Bay Area's Farmland ($4.00)
3. Bay Area Agricultural Production Issues (full report $8.00; summary report $2.00)
4. Bay Area Farmland Loss: Trends and Case Studies($4.00)
5. Protecting the Region's Farmland: Governmental Policies and Alternatives ($4.00)
6. The Impact of a Bay Area Farmbelt on Urban Development (Discussion paper; write for availability)

TECHNICAL MEMOS
2a. Agricultural Employment in the Bay Area ($1.00)
2b. Bay Area Direct Marketing Survey ($1.00)
2c. Community Traditions in Bay Area Agriculture ($1.00)
2d. Social and Economic Diversity in Bay Area Agriculture ($1.00)
2e. Water Resources and Agricultural Land Use ($1.00)
2f. Agricultural Land and Wildlife Resources in the Bay Area ($1.00)

3a. The Bay Area Agricultural Real Estate Market (draft — $4.00)
4a. Bay Area Farmland Loss Projections, 1975-2000 ($1.00)

SPECIAL STUDIES
1. The Williamson Act After Proposition 13 ($2.00)
2. California Agricultural Zoning ($2.00)
3. The Productivity of Bay Area Rangeland ($2.00)
4. Analysis of Ranchland Zoning Policies (write for availability)

OTHER PUBLICATIONS
Regional Exchange newsletters: Bay Area Agriculture. An Overview (Jan. 1980); Farmland Loss — A Nationwide Problem (April 1980); Farmland Loss — A Regional Problem (July 1980); Oregon's Farmland Preservation Program (Fall 1980)
"Bay Area Agriculture — Its High Productivity, Its Precarious Future" (**Cry California** article, Summer 1980)
"Farmers Who Are Holding On" (**California Living**, May 4, 1980)
All of these publications are free; a self addressed, first class stamped envelope is requested.

In addition to these written reports, a separate project to identify on maps the region's productive agricultural lands was undertaken. No publication of this data was prepared.

The Farmlands Project made use of two reports published earlier: ABAG's **Agricultural Resources Study** (1969); and McDonald and Associates', **The Impact of the Sonoma County General Plan on Agriculture and Land Use** (Sonoma County, 1978). The latter study was especially helpful in framing parts of our economic analysis.

The project was supervised by the POS committee listed at the front of the report. This committee met every month over the course of the project to review the work products and to provide overall policy direction. In addition, many committee members participated in other project-related meetings.

In addition, a Farmlands Citizen Advisory Group met ten times during the project to consider and offer advice on the policy recommendations of the report. Members included:

Dorothy Erskine, POS Project Committee
Bob Girard, Santa Clara County
Ralph Grossi, Marin County
Mariska Huynen, San Mateo County
Cynthia Kay, Terry Rogers; Solano County
T. J. Kent, Jr., Co-chairman,
   POS Project Committee
Elizabeth Kilham, Contra Costa County
Brad Lundborg, Co-chairman,
   Sonoma County
Art Paull, Alameda County
Lennie Roberts, San Mateo County
Karin Urquhart, Marin County
Ciddy Wordell, Santa Clara County

STAFF, CONSULTANTS & ACKNOWLEDGEMENTS

PROJECT STAFF

Larry Orman, POS Executive Director, directed the Farmlands Project.

Marianne Constable was in charge of office and financial management, in addition to undertaking research and analysis on the zoning survey special study. Because of her capable and conscientious administration, the project was able to be conducted with exceptional efficiency.

Meredith Tromble and Lisa Tidball served as administrative assistants. Both Lisa and Meredith made it possible to complete the large number of project reports by putting in extensive extra effort.

The project background reports were developed primarily by the research associates who worked at different times for the project: Pamela Westing (Background Report #4); Richard Osborn (Background Report #3); and Ralph Mead (Background Reports #2 and #6). Dan Marks was in charge of the mapping project and helped coordinate much of the field work in the latter part of the project. Each of these staff members did thoroughly professional work under very difficult time deadlines, and deserve special credit for their efforts.

Four research assistants contributed to the project over the two years: Marty Roberts (Rangeland Special Study), Tom Bassett (Background Reports #1 and #2 technical memos), Pam Ricci (mapping), and Pat Young (mapping and general research). As with the regular project staff, each of these research assistants brought a great deal of care and enthusiasm to their work.

Volunteer assistance was provided by several people, especially Kathie Casey of San Francisco State University on the mapping project, and Jonathan Levine of U.C. Berkeley on the Williamson Act Study. Jeanette Young, Abraham Rosoff, and Jack Sobiloff also helped with the mapping work. In addition, Priscilla Partridge and John Papagni contributed generously of their time on specific research tasks.

PROJECT CONSULTANTS

Early in the project, we were fortunate to have L. T. Wallace of the U.C. Cooperative Extension agree to serve as a policy consultant. Tim's experience as former head of the State Department of Food and Agriculture and with the University was extremely useful in shaping much of our research.

Prior to becoming Executive Director of the California Public Utilities Commission, Joe Bodovitz also served as a project policy consultant and assisted in the work program development and in formulation of the recommendations; he then continued with the project, serving on the supervising committee.

John Hart was selected as the writing consultant for the project, and prepared the text of the final report as well as several articles. John's ability to transform technical information into clean and lively narrative was invaluable.

To advise on legal aspects of our policy recommendations, we relied on Michael B. Wilmar, who is also the Executive Director of the Bay Conservation and Development Commission. Michael's understanding of the practicalities of the regulatory process was crucial to our recommendations for a special Agricultural Land Commission.

Bob Twiss, now Chairman of the Tahoe Regional Planning Agency and on the faculty of U.C. Berkeley, also advised on legal and policy matters, especially regarding our mapping.

For development of our educational program for the news media, Ken McEldowney served as consultant. Ken also made important contributions to the structure and approach of the final report.

ACKNOWLEDGEMENTS

In conducting the Farmlands Project, we received the cooperation of many, many people — farmers, public officials and agency staff, private consultants, university faculty, and private citizens. To all, we wish to extend our thanks; without such helpful assistance, the Farmlands Project would have been a less productive effort. Specifically, however, the following people were especially generous in giving their time and knowledge:

Professor James Bartoleme, U.C. Berkeley
Dr. Rick Bennett, Sonoma County Farm
   Advisor's Office
Bill Bruner, U.S. Soil Conservation Service,
   Contra Costa County
Tim Caulkins, Solano County
   Planning Department
California Department of Water Resources,
   Central Division — Wayne MacRostie, Chief
George Constent, San Francisco
   Produce Terminal
Perry Davilla, Rancher
Nona Dennis, Madrone Associates
Peter Detweiler, State Office
   of Planning and Research
John Duffy, Sonoma County Farm Bureau
Ron Eber, Oregon Land Conservation
   and Development Commission
Charles O. Forester, ABAG
Bruce Freeland, Cheriel Jensen;
   Santa Clara County Planning Department
Bruce Fry, Gerry Wallace;
   Alameda County Planning Department
George Goldman, Kirby Moulton;
   U.C. Cooperative Extension, Berkeley
Gordon Gram, British Columbia
   Agricultural Land Commission
Kathleen Hagerty, Federal Reserve Bank
Jeff Jacobs, California State Bureau
   of Direct Marketing
Warren Johnston, Robert Hagan, U.C.
   Cooperative Extension, Davis
David Katz, Center for Sustainable Agriculture
Walter Kieser, McDonald and Associates
Dr. Bill Kortum, Petaluma
Starker Leopold, U.C. Berkeley
Dr. Phillip LeVeen, U.C. Berkeley
Jack Liebster, Joe Nicholson;
   California Coastal Commission

Charles Little, American Land Forum
Tony McClimans, Napa County
   Planning Department
Michael Nash, Calif. Cooperative Creamery
Erik Nikerson, Bank of America
Dr. Richard Norgaard, U.C. Berkeley
Harry Reeves, East Bay Regional Park District
Richard Rominger, Secretary,
   State Department of Food and Agriculture
Dale Sanders, Contra Costa County
   Planning Department
Henry Schacht, Calif. Canners and Growers
Helene Swenerton, U.C. Cooperative Extension
Lasta Tomasevich, Marin County
   Planning Department
Carol Whitmire, Sonoma County
   Planning Department
Charles Wollenberg, Laney College

Finally, and certainly not least, we wish to acknowledge with special thanks the support and participation of Roberta Mundie of Gruen, Gruen + Associates, and George Sato of the California Department of Water Resources. Roberta and George were both invaluable, particularly in the early stages of the project and in their reviews of our background reports.

Bibliography

The following are reports and sources for additional information on agriculture and farmland projects. For a more detailed listing of sources, see individual POS Farmlands Project reports.

Lester R. Brown **The Worldwide Loss of Cropland**. Washington: Worldwatch Institute, 1978.

Charles E. Little, editor **Land and Food: The Preservation of U.S. Farmland**. Washington: American Land Forum, 1979.

Max Schnepf, editor **Farmland, Food and the Future**. Iowa: Soil Conservation Society of America, 1979.

Available from: SCSA, 7515 N. Ankeny Rd., Ankeny, IA 50021.

Lyle Schertz , et. al. **Another Revolution in U.S. Farming?** Washington: U.S. Department of Agriculture, 1979.

Leonard U. Wilson **State Agricultural Land Issues**. Kentucky: Council of State Governments, 1979.

Available from: Council of State Govts., Iron Works Pike, Lexington, KY 40578.

ORGANIZATIONS:

American Land Forum, 1025 Vermont Ave. NW, Washington DC 20005.
Conducts policy research on land use issues nationwide.

National Agricultural Lands Study, New EOB, 722 Jackson Pl. NW, Washington DC 20006.
Two-year study by federal government, due to report in early 1981.

Farmlands Preservation Institute, 9107 E. Parkhill Dr., Bethesda, MD 20014.
Publishes **FPI Survey** newsletter.

National Assoc. of Counties Research Foundation **Agricultural Lands Project**, 1735 New York Ave. NW, Washington DC 20006.
Publishes **Ag Lands Exchange** newsletter and **Disappearing Farmlands** brochure.

People for Open Space

People for Open Space is a non-profit organization established in 1958. Over the past two decades, POS has helped conservationists and other civic leaders in the nine-county Bay Area develop common policies and exchange information, and has carried out its own educational programs about the regional planning and open space preservation needs of the Bay Area. In order to help dramatize the need for and importance of such efforts, we prepared **The Case for Open Space** in 1969, a foundation financed study of the costs and benefits of a permanent open space system. This unique study was undertaken with foundation support and demonstrated the economic feasibility of a permanent Bay Area greenbelt. We have also sponsored over 20 regional conferences and publish the quarterly **Regional Exchange** newsletter.

People for Open Space is a membership organization, and we hope you will join us in our efforts to protect the productive agricultural and other open space lands of the San Francisco Bay Area.

People for Open Space
46 Kearny Street
San Francisco, CA 94108
(415) 781-8729